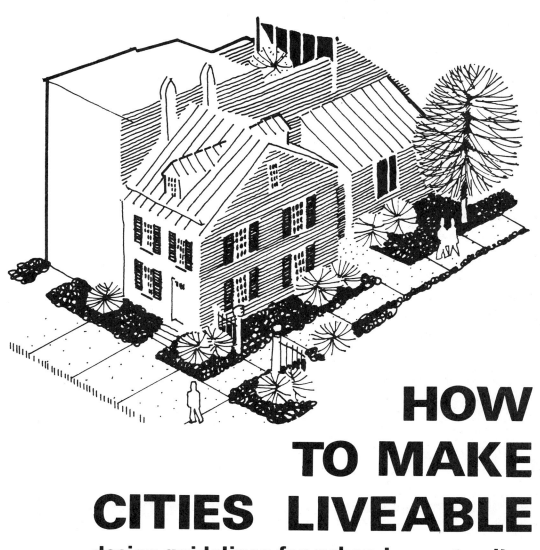

HOW
TO MAKE
CITIES LIVEABLE
design guidelines for urban homesteading

Environmental Design Press
Edited by Gary O. Robinette

VNR **VAN NOSTRAND REINHOLD COMPANY**

How to Make Cities Liveable

Copyright © 1984 by Van Nostrand Reinhold Company Inc.

Library of Congress Catalog Card Number 84-10393

ISBN 0-442-22203-3

Printed in the United States of America

Published by Van Nostrand Reinhold Company Inc.
135 West 50th Street
New York, New York 10020

Van Nostrand Reinhold Company Limited
Molly Millars Lane
Wokingham, Berkshire RG11 2PY, England

Van Nostrand Reinhold
480 La Trobe Street
Melbourne, Victoria 3000, Australia

Macmillan of Canada
Division of Gage Publishing Limited
164 Commander Boulevard
Agincourt, Ontario M1S 3C7, Canada

16 15 14 13 12 11 10 9 8 7 6 5 4 3 2 1

Library of Congress Cataloging in Publication Data
Main entry under title:

How to make cities liveable.

 Based on three summary reports prepared by the staff of Land Design/Research, Inc. of Columbia, Md.
  Bibliography: p.
  Includes index.
  1. Architecture, Domestic—Maryland—Baltimore—Conservation and restoration. 2. Community development, Urban—Maryland—Baltimore. 3. Urban beautification—Maryland—Baltimore. 4. Architecture—Maryland—Baltimore—Human factors. I. Robinette, Gary O. II. Land Design/Research, Inc.
NA7238.B3H69   1984   728.3'12   84-10393
ISBN 0-442-22203-3

How To Make Cities Liveable

Edited by Gary O. Robinette

This book is excerpted from and is based on the following publications:

Otterbein Homestead Area
Guidelines for Exterior Restoration

Prepared by:

Land Design/Research, Inc.
Columbia, Maryland

Client:

Charles Center Inner Harbor Management, Inc.

Department of Housing and Community Development
City of Baltimore

Guidelines for Barre Circle Homestead Area

Prepared by:

Land Design/Research, Inc.
Columbia, Maryland

In cooperation with:

Barre Circle Homesteaders
Baltimore, Maryland

Under contract with:

Department of Housing and Community Development
City of Baltimore

Table of Contents

Preface

This is not a book about townhouses, or about architectural styles, or facades, or window openings or even about environmental or site design. It is not even a book about Baltimore. It **is** a book about **how** to make cities truly liveable; economically, socially, politically and environmentally. This book tells part of the story about how two inner city neighborhoods in Baltimore, Maryland were guided toward renovation, restoration and new life through an innovative public-private partnership. In doing that, it provides a guide as to how many other older cities can be made liveable, affordable and pleasant as well as economically, socially and environmentally sound.

The urban homesteading program in Baltimore and in many other cities is an exciting concept. The award-winning studies on which this book is based were exciting and the actual result in providing affordable housing in the Baltimore Inner Harbor is even more exciting. This particular book has been put together to show what was done by the consultants for the local residents on behalf of the City and other sponsors to help in restoring and renovating individual rowhouses and the entire neighborhood. Obviously all parts of this program could not be utilized and applied intact in Terra Haute or Trenton or in any other specific city. However, the basic principles, the approach and the methodology used by the staff of Land Design/Research would work in any number of other local neighborhoods in many cities with very sensitive and careful adaptation to local conditions.

This book is based on a series of three books or summary reports of studies prepared by the staff of Land Design/Research, Inc. of Columbia, Maryland for various governmental and private entities in the City of Baltimore and in the State of Maryland. The text and illustrations from these summary reports have been edited and pulled together into this one book to illustrate the approach and the method used in Baltimore which could be used in other communities to make cities generally more liveable. Because of the derivation of the material in this book there are some discontinuities and a certain amount of disjointedness. The summary report on the Otterbein Homestead Area was typeset and bound with extensive graphic design and with a number of photographs. The summary report on the Barre Circle Homestead Area was hand lettered and did not contain any photographs. The Barre Circle report was also bound in a 3-ring binder so that the local residents and consultants could insert additional material and use it as a living, growing and working document. The Barre Circle report was completed after the Otterbein study and borrowed extensively from this earlier report. The Barre Circle report did amplify certain areas of interest beyond those contained in the Otterbein report. This book consolidates and integrates both of those volumes. Logistically this is both difficult and evident as seen in the final result. The Barre Circle drawings are much more loose and are usually captioned by hand. There is some duplication of text, but Barre Circle basically amplifies and expands on the earlier work of the Otterbein project. The Otterbein study contained a separate section on site considerations and energy conservation while the Barre Circle study contained a further amplification of guidelines for fencing and an extensive overview of environmental considerations and a discussion of the use of color in various areas in the project. The third volume in the series was entitled, *Housing Rehabilitation Preservation,* and was prepared by the same consultants for the Maryland Department of Economic and Community Development. No material in this book was taken from that study, but it did amplify on the guidelines for the two homesteading areas with information on how, legally and financially, to bring some parts of this program into reality in other situations and locations.

The final product of restored and renewed neighborhoods in Baltimore is seen to be very successful from the vantage point of 10 years after the initiation and inception of the program. The publications on which this book is based must be given credit as a part of the underlying reason for that success. Obviously the renovation, restoration and design guidelines illustrated in this book are not the sole reason for the success of the Baltimore urban homesteading program. There were many other factors which contributed, but these carefully delineated, illustrated and understandable guidelines **were** a significant part of the overall program which included very strong support from the public and private leadership in Baltimore. The program would not have been nearly as successful without the design guidelines and the communication tool they provided.

The essence of these guidelines for application in other situations by environmental designers and administrators involves the following points:

What aspects should be included in the development of such guidelines?

In what form can they be most effectively and understandably communicated?

How do you balance the degree of guidance and suggestion to avoid dictating and yet allow for individual discretion and expression?

These are not minimum property standards, but design assistance, made available to a large group all at one time to insure quality and unity. Individual architectural and site design would have been inordinately expensive for a homeowner who had just bought an abandoned shell for $1.00 and had only two years to bring the property up to standards. These guidelines were a way that all of these new homeowners could be given assistance and guidance for a reasonable cost. The guidelines helped to provide a unity to the completed neighborhood. This entire program was very practical and realistic and has been accepted and utilized in a remarkable way over a period of time. There have been all too few successes in making cities liveable in the past few decades. These are guidelines and this is a program that worked:

it provided pleasant and safe streets where there were abandoned, boarded up, rat-infested building shells near the center of the city,

it provided new taxes for the city at little cost to the city and provided an upgrading of the neighborhood and reasonably priced homes to those who were able to provide "sweat equity" for an economically sound investment for everyone,

it provided a sense of place in that, socially, the residents are **a part of the city, not apart from the city** as is so often the case in low rent or in public housing projects,

it provided measurable environmental improvement with extensive planting and a unified quality through coordinated paving and construction materials.

Hopefully this book will make this information available to a wider audience beyond the residents of these two neighborhoods in Baltimore. In doing that it may be of assistance to others in other situations and circumstances in making cities liveable.

Gary O. Robinette
Editor

Introduction

Area history

In 1785, the existing Old Otterbein Church was built. It later was named for its first pastor Rev. Philip Wilhelm Otterbein.

The area around the church, now called Old Otterbein, was the site of homes owned by some of Baltimore's renowned merchants such as Moses Sheppard and Enoch Pratt, men whose substantial fortunes elevated the City to the status of a world port. Several generals of the War of 1812 also lived on South Charles Street near the Otterbein neighborhood.

Here, close by the once bustling Light and Pratt Street wharves, the commission merchants and bankers lived, keeping an eye on their inventories of tobacco, spices, teas, coffees, sugar, molasses, dry goods, lumber and fruits. They built simple, wide and substantial brick houses, designed as cleanly as were the lines of their sailing ships. Here lived the middlemen, the traders and capitalists who stood between Fells Point's mariners and the American South and West where Baltimore sold her goods.

Otterbein was also home to the merchant's employees and tradespeople, those who kept the ledgers, loomed the wool, brewed the beer and laid the bricks during Baltimore's early growth years.

The homes, shops and workrooms of the tradespeople were built in the same blocks as those of the merchants. Tucked away in little back or side alleys, like Welcome, Homespun and Honey, other dwellings bespeak a time when the City was not economically segregated. During the first half of the 19th century, freed blacks lived alongside whites, in a city loosely segregated by occupation rather than economic station or race. Today, there are magnificent homes scattered throughout the Old Otterbein neighborhood. Many seem to have once had side gardens. The homes opened on large, common squares, backyard breathing spaces that contained an amazing collection of walls and servant quarters.

In the same neighborhood is the Old Marburg Tobacco Company building, at Charles and Camden Street. This 1887 structure, designed by architect Charles

Otterbein site location

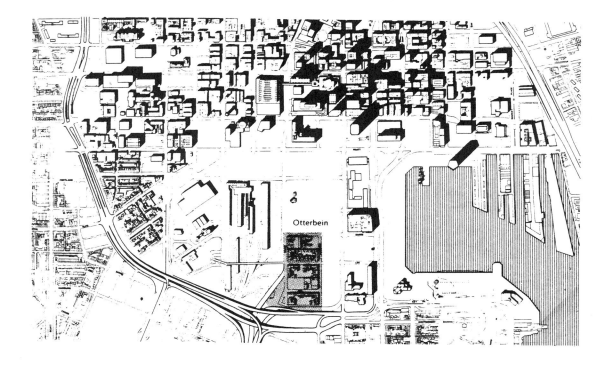

Otterbein

How to Make Cities Liveable

Carson has granite swirling detail work, archways and windows decorated in the Adler-Sullivan, Chicago style of architecture. Farther west is Camden Station, the 1857 depot that was once the main Baltimore terminal for the B & O railroad. Though modified over the years, it remains a handsome brick building with a golden oak interior.

The Old Otterbein neighborhood's unique role in the economic and social history of Baltimore, its relationship to the Inner Harbor and downtown, and the existing qualities of the homes themselves and the surrounding historic buildings are some of the characteristics making the area worthy of preservation and restoration. Although the Otterbein Homestead Area is not the first concentrated homesteading area in Baltimore, it is certainly the most notable and unique.

Otterbein project location

The Otterbein Homestead site is a 2½ city block area approximately 4 blocks from downtown Baltimore, bordered by Barre Street on the north, Hanover Street on the east, Hughes Street on the south and Sharp Street on the west. The site is east of the Camden Railroad yards, west of the Inner Harbor Project I and a part of the Inner Harbor West Residential Development Plan.

Originally, the 130 structures were to be torn down to make way for more modern residential units. However, the intense public interest in the homesteading program, and the historical significance of the Otterbein neighborhood, persuaded the City to modify the master plan to include the homesteading approach.

Even though the Otterbein Homesteading Area is no longer the largest homesteading area in Baltimore, it is the one located closest to the Inner Harbor and downtown Baltimore with its shopping, governmental and cultural and tourist facilities. Within the site are approximately 105 houses which have been designated for single family occupancy. In addition, approximately 20 other buildings are planned for multi-family development or other uses. There are also par-cels of cleared land designated for some form of future development. The diversity of unit types and future development potential makes this project unique.

Barre Circle project location

The Barre Circle Homestead Area is part of a three block area approximately 7 blocks from downtown Baltimore, bordered by Lombard Street on the north, the East-West Boulevard on the east, Ramsey Street on the south, and Scott Street on the west. The site is within a ½ mile radius of downtown Baltimore's retail and business center, the Inner Harbor, and the University of Maryland at Baltimore, immediately to the northeast.

The Barre Circle Homestead Area has the largest number of homesteading units of any project in Baltimore. Within the site are approximately 150 rowhouses which have been designated for single family occupancy. There are also parcels of cleared land to be allocated for landscaping and community space.

Homesteading

The concept of homesteading was used over 100 years ago as a means of promoting the development of the Western United States. Under the Federal Homestead and Extension Law of 1862, a citizen could obtain up to 160 acres of public land by paying a nominal registration fee. Under this law, millions of acres of land

Barre Circle site location

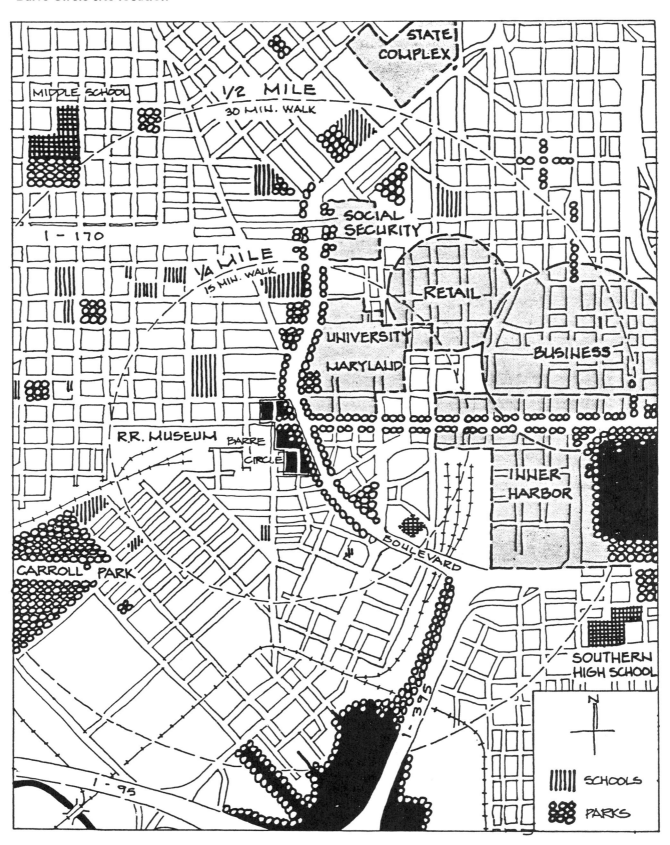

were given to settlers who lived on the land and cultivated it for five years.

The original concept has been modified today to promote the rehabilitation of vacant and neglected houses in urban areas. Baltimore was one of the first cities in the country to use homesteading to revitalize declining neighborhoods. The first property under the Baltimore Homesteading Program was awarded in 1974. Since that time, over one hundred dwellings have been rehabilitated through homesteading.

Properties are selected for homesteading by the Department of Housing and Community Development from among those acquired by the city. The public is notified of the availability of properties and can apply to the Department of Housing and Community Development for a specific property. One applicant is selected for each property either by a committee or through a lottery as was the case with the Otterbein project.

A cost estimate for the revitalization of the property is obtained and the homesteader has the opportunity to borrow money from the City at a less than market interest rate for the rehabilitation work required.

The homesteader must satisfy certain fire and safety requirements and agree to move into the property within 6 months after rehabilitation work starts.

Within two years from the signing of the homestead agreement, the property must be certified as meeting all applicable code standards. The homesteader then obtains title to the property from the City.

The homesteading program requires a commitment both by the City and by the homesteader in order to be successful. The program, however, provides benefits not only to the City and the homesteader, but also to the surrounding community as well. Some of the specific benefits of the homesteading program are:

1. It recycles a neglected segment of the available housing in the community and puts abandoned dwellings back into use and on the tax rolls.

2. It contributes to the revitalization of declining neighborhoods by encouraging improvements to both the immediate residential area and the surrounding community.

3. It increases the opportunity for home ownership to families and individuals who otherwise might not be eligible.

4. It provides residential neighborhoods which are convenient to downtown cultural facilities and places of work.

5. It makes available older houses with varied architectural details and lower square foot cost than many new houses.

Project objectives

The objectives of this project are to create a viable urban residential neighborhood which will preserve and enhance its positive qualities and at the same time function as an integral part of the Inner Harbor West Development Area. This is to be accomplished through the development of neighborhood plans for the restoration of public areas and through the development of exterior restoration guidelines for the buildings.

Although the Otterbein Homestead Area contains the essential elements necessary for a successful revitalization, a thoughtful, comprehensive, and cooperative planning effort is necessary in order to achieve this end. The comprehensive planning effort is intended to:

1. **develop a master plan and site development plans for the renewal and revitalization of the existing structures and public spaces of Otterbein.**

2. **develop plans for this historic area that are consistent with the larger framework of the total community plan for the Inner Harbor West Area.**

3. **develop a system of exterior design guidelines that are clear, educative and informative in nature rather than a mandatory list of requirements.**

4. develop a system which deals with all exterior elements of the buildings rather than just street front facades.

5. provide for the direct participation by the future residents of the Otterbein Homesteading Area in the site development planning and the exterior guideline formation.

6. create a system of guidelines that will assist the resident's architectural review committee in monitoring and upholding the environmental quality of the Otterbein Homesteading Area.

Although the concept of homesteading is fairly simple, the execution of a successful project such as Otterbein is quite complex. A successful transformation of the neighborhood will require careful and sensitive rehabilitation efforts by both the City and the residents. Because of the need for direct resident involvement and the complexity of the project, the City encouraged resident participation in the planning process. The participation has been beneficial since it has made the residents more aware of the need for standards and guidelines, and a continuing neighborhood involvement.

Neighborhood Plan

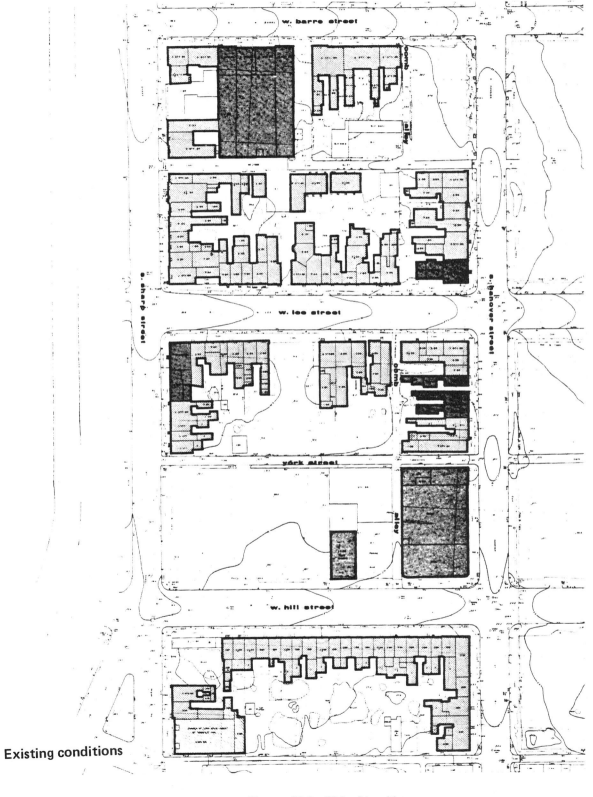

Existing conditions

The development intent of the Otterbein Homestead Area has been to integrate the existing structures and vacant lands into a contiguous and unified neighborhood.

From a physical point of view a neighborhood is an area which takes advantage of its location and relationship with the rest of the City and its activities while at the same time maintaining a separate identity. This definition of the neighborhood has two aspects. First, there is the external aspect which relates it to the rest of the City. Secondly, there is the internal aspect in which it maintains a separate identity.

External Considerations

The external considerations are those aspects which relate or link Otterbein to the Inner Harbor Area and the rest of the City. The external considerations important to Otterbein may be listed under the following headings: vehicular access; pedestrian linkages; view/vistas; and adjacent development.

Vehicular access

The Otterbein Homestead Area lies in the southwest corner of the Inner Harbor West plan. Present planning calls for vehicular access on the north at Barre Street and on the east at Hanover Street. The proposed Interstate 395 and City Boulevard will make access to the **west** and to the **south** less direct.

Direct egress from Otterbein to the Interstate system and to the south will be limited to one point at the northwest corner of the site at the intersection of Barre and Sharp Street. Vehicular access to downtown Baltimore and to the north will be through the Inner Harbor West development.

Although the proposed Interstate 395 to the west and the south will edge the project, it has been proposed that the alignment be shifted in order to allow for a minimum of 60 to 70 feet of landscaped buffer between the existing edges of Sharp and Hughes Street and the highway system. Such a buffer will not only help provide a visual and sound barrier for Otterbein, but will also create a meaningful landscaped edge to the homestead area.

Pedestrian linkages

The major pedestrian movement from Otterbein will be north to the northern portion of the Inner Harbor West development area and downtown Baltimore, and east to the Inner Harbor. The proposed plan allows for pedestrian linkage to the north to be provided along Hanover Street.

Two traffic lanes will remain open with 18-20' wide sidewalks and plantings on both edges. Direct pedestrian linkage to the east and the Harbor will be provided along the existing alignment of Hill Street. Hill Street will be closed to vehicular traffic and will be paved and planted as a major pedestrian walkway.

View/vistas

The east-west streets through Otterbein are oriented to allow views toward the harbor. As the land slopes gradually toward the water, some interesting vistas currently exist along W. Hill, W. Lee and W. Barre Streets. It is hoped that the future development to the east of Otterbein will be so designed and located to maintain these existing views of the harbor area.

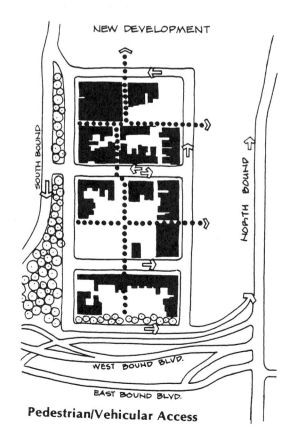

Pedestrian/Vehicular Access

Adjacent development

In order to create a gradual transition in architectural style and to relate in scale to the restored units of Otterbein, it has been suggested that future development to the east be a maximum of three stories in height. It has also been proposed that the future units to the east and north of Otterbein be compatible in terms of scale, materials, color, detailing, and density to conform to the overall character of the Otterbein Homestead Area. This is especially important for new development facing onto S. Hanover Street and W. Barre Street.

Internal Considerations

The internal considerations are those aspects which affect Otterbein within the project boundaries. Such internal considerations are vehicular circulation, parking, pedestrian circulation, property ownership, multi-family/community facilities and infill development.

Vehicular circulation

Although the Otterbein neighborhood is being planned with emphasis on the pedestrian, the automobile must be recognized as an important part of modern life. If the vehicular circulation scheme is properly designed, the automobile can have a positive impact on an urban residential neighborhood. Many existing neighborhoods within Baltimore can be used as a model to illustrate this fact.

In order to minimize traffic flow within the homestead area and discourage through traffic from surrounding areas, a one-way traffic system has been developed.

The one-way system will allow for adequate internal circulation on streets of appropriate width and scale. The one-way roads also allow for the existing sidewalks to be widened and enable easier pedestrian circulation.

Vista - Toward the Inner Harbor

Proposed infill architecture, corner Barre Circle and Hanover Street

Proposed community building and recreation space

How to Make Cities Liveable

Any newly constructed residential units should be compatible with the restored units, in order to create a consistency throughout the Otterbein neighborhood.

Pedestrian circulation

In an urban neighborhood such as Otterbein major emphasis should be placed on pedestrian circulation and activity. The narrowing of existing streets as proposed will enable sidewalks to be widened and allow for planting to provide a more attractive pedestrian environment. This will make the area more conducive to walking and biking. It is also recommended that pedestrian crossing areas be enlarged to encourage ease of movement and create a safer pedestrian environment. These enlarged crossing areas will be provided at points where the internal pathway crosses a street and also at the corners of blocks. At the corners the enlargements also serve to create a more enclosed or private entry feeling to the street.

The creation of internal pedestrian walkways linking all elements of the neighborhood is another major factor in creating a desirable pedestrian environment. The concept for the design of the pedestrian walkway system is to provide ease of access from the homes to the community open space, to allow rear yard service and and provide for emergency needs. The plan proposes utilization of existing alleyways such as Welcome, York and Comb, as major pedestrian linkages and service ways. New pedestrian walkways will be provided from the alleyways to the rear of the residential units.

Multi-family/Community facilities

The proposed site development plan recognizes the potential of both those units allocated for multi-family development as well as those unallocated structures. One of the unallocated structures, the church on Hill Street, is currently being used as a tire sales facility. It has been designated as a potential community facility.

It is also the recommendation that all multi-family structures as well as many proposed new residential units be subjected to rigorous design guidelines that will ensure their compatibility with the restored single family units.

Summary of the Plan

The proposed neighborhood plan is intended to create an urban residential neighborhood that generates pride and care from its inhabitants, is contiguous in character, is primarily

pedestrian oriented, has limited vehicular traffic and creates a high-quality environment through comprehensive landscape design.

The specific elements of the plan are as follows:

A. **Narrowing of the existing streets and the widening of sidewalks.**

B. **Introduction of street trees and other planting throughout the neighborhood.**

C. **Parking to be primarily accommodated on-street.**

D. **Existing alleyways with their granite block surfaces to be retained as pedestrian walkways allowing for emergency vehicle and service access.**

E. **Small pedestrian walkways to connect units to the major pedestrian ways and to provide rear yard access for service.**

F. **Internal landscaped open spaces for active and passive use.**

G. **Infill development for new single family rowhouses in most vacant areas to complement the existing character of the restored units.**

H. **New sidewalks with consistent site detailing and furnishings.**

I. **Sidewalks widened at points of pedestrian crossing.**

J. **Landscape buffer zones to be provided along west and south edges of the neighborhood.**

The primary image of row housing is its block face. Few buildings are visually prominent either through flamboyance of style, irregularity of form or marked difference in materials. It is important to emphasize that each residential unit is part of a larger architectural facade. A sensitivity to the overall appearance of the block face is essential in renovating each unit, as a complementary part of the larger whole.

The ability to address the whole block as a single entity cannot be overstressed. The inter-relationship of elements which when combined create the overall block character should be the primary concern when evaluating exterior modifications. A positive architectural facade

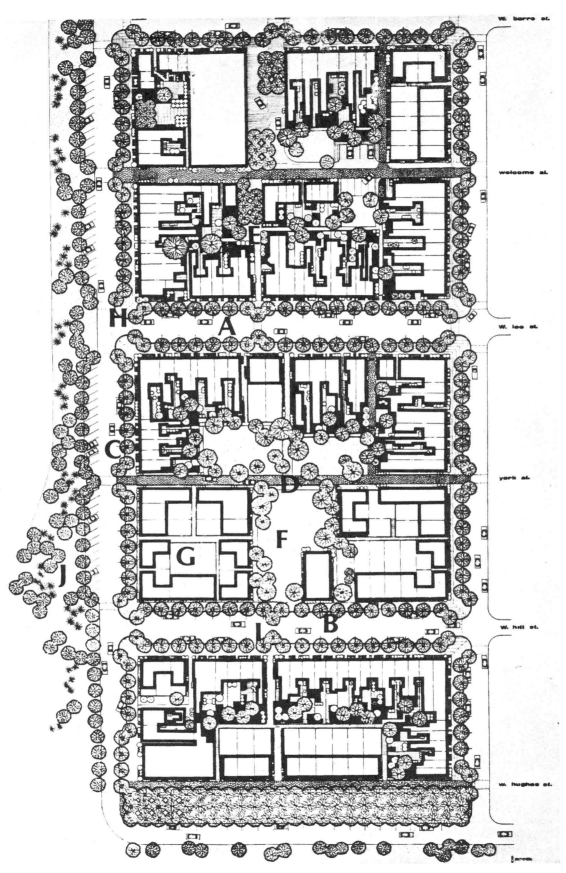

Neighborhood development plan

How to Make Cities Liveable

Parking

The alternatives of on-street parking and off-street parking were explored. On-street parking provides for the dual use of existing streets as both a thoroughfare and a parking area. This alternative was selected because it allowed utilization of existing street patterns and eliminated the need to create large internal parking lots.

The proposed plan indicates that the majority of parking will be on-street and supplemented by minimal internal parking along the mid-block alleyways in the higher density zones. Those alleyways will be retained as internal emergency and service access areas. By providing a parking ratio of 1 to 1:3 spaces per unit, the plan allows for the majority of the spaces to be provided in the public right of ways rather then utilizing valuable internal land for parking. This enables the internal vacant land to be utilized for community use or new infill development.

Property ownership

The allocation of property ownership is a significant factor in structuring the neighborhood plan. Various alternatives for ownership exist ranging from all land outside of building walls being quasi-public or in community ownership to the total land being divided into individual lots and held in private ownership. Obviously, there are benefits and also disadvantages associated with each extreme.

Typical property distribution

If all land outside of building walls was held in common ownership, there would be no immediate private areas outside the home, no pride of ownership or sense of responsibility for the areas adjacent to one's home. There would also be no transition between the privacy inside one's home and the more public areas immediately outside. On the other hand, if all the land within the project were carved up by private ownership, it would create an inequitable distribution of land among homesteaders. It would also be an inappropriate use of valuable, urban land eliminating the possibility of any community space.

The general objective in allocating ownership was to provide for an equitable distribution of property, one that satifies not only individual homeowner's needs for private outdoor areas, but also satisfies the neighborhood's needs for circulation space, community activity space, and appropriate infill development.

Infill development

A key concept of the plan is to utilize much of the existing vacant lands for infill residential development compatible with the restored units. The vacant land, particularly those parcels at the edges of the blocks, creates a feeling of an unstable or changing neighborhood. It also conveys the image of piecemeal development. The infilling of the block spaces will not only unify the individual blocks, but also recognizes the City's desire to create new housing opportunities in the inner city on valuable urban land. The plan also proposes some minimal infill development on the internal portions of the blocks, particularly in the mid and south block. These units are to be of consistent character and scale with the existing internal units on Welcome Alley.

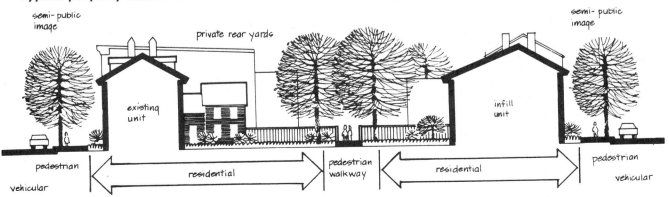

Architectural
considerations

The architectural character of the Otterbein Homestead Area is determined by:

1. the interrelationship of architectural elements that make up the individual units and,
2. the units themselves in combination with one another that create the overall block character.

It is essential to understand these relationships in order to provide the basis from which residents can proceed with their own individual analyses and subsequent restorations.

The approach followed in the creation of architectural guidelines was first to inventory the indigenous architectural elements that form the character of Otterbein, analyze those characteristics and prepare guidelines that are sensitive to their restoration. The following process was utilized:

I. DETERMINE AND INVENTORY THE EXISTING ARCHITECTURAL CHARACTERISTICS

This was accomplished by various site visits, photographic evaluation of all block faces within the project, and architectural and historical research to determine the various architectural styles.

II. ANALYZE THE CHARACTERISTICS

This was accomplished by a block-by-block architectural evaluation, individual unit evaluations, and visits to other historic revitalization projects.

III. PREPARE GUIDELINES FOR RE—STORATION

This was accomplished by preparing draft guidelines, meeting with residents and the City, and compiling the final publication.

Block Considerations

The architecture of the Otterbein district is generally restrained and dignified. Few buildings are visually prominent either through flamboyance of style, irregularity of form or marked differentiation of materials.

Most buildings are of similar form, scale, proportions, color and texture. Although variations do exist, the traditional Otterbein rowhouse is constructed of brick, two or three stories high, placed perpendicularly to the street, attached on both sides, aligned at the front property line and crowned with either a pitched roof or flat cornice.

It is important to emphasize that each specific living unit is a part of a larger building group. A sensitivity to the overall design of that building group is essential in restoring each unit as a complementary part of a larger whole.

Visual continuity through consistent design elements is important to the block and neighborhood image and can reintroduce the art of architectural courtesy; that is, a sensitivity of how one unit can complement and be complemented by adjacent units. Architectural courtesy and sensitivity are not accomplished by mere restrictive or mandatory statements but by an understanding of the elements which help determine the character and quality of each block.

Forms

A typical block of Otterbein may be viewed as one solid building or a series of abutting buildings.

The block face is formed by an aligned front of similar rectangular forms of two to three story and 10-24' wide rectangles. Those rectangles are differentiated by slightly varying color in brick, abutting wall joints, random termination of heights, and random levels of window groupings.

A major element of the forms is the triangular shape of pitched roofs, the intense articulation of the cornices and fascias and the commercial fronts which are applied to the buildings. In some instances, the stoop and entrance areas also provide some relief from the flat quality of the block face.

Roofscape

The roofscape is composed of the chimneys, dormers, cornices, pitched roofs, and the skyline. It is a collection of rectangular, sharp edged and pitched roof forms and dark colors and random patterns. The randomness and variety is an obvious relief to the more evenly aligned front facades, and provides a variety not normally found in contiguous units of rowhouses.

Texture

Texture may be defined as the arrangement, size and quantity of repeated elements of the block facades of Otterbein. (More repeated elements equals greater sense of texture).

The texture of a block is created by the uniform and numerous bricks, the random placement of window groupings, rectilinear and vertical in emphasis, the rhythmic series of doors and stoops, the scattered pattern of lintels and sills, and the cornices.

Function

It is important to understand how the block as a unit and the individual buildings were originally used and how that use reflected the traditional daily activity.

Units were oriented towards the street with the public facade and main entrance on the street. Private areas were in the rear with service access from alleyways. Major light sources were in the front and rear of the units and partial basements were often created, thus requiring stairs to enter on the first floor. Shutters and blinds were often employed for ventilation and security.

Open spaces

The city blocks of Otterbein do not present a solid, unending veneer of architecture. The blocks are interrupted by alleyways, streets and occasional units with side yards.

The alleyways and small streets provide access to the rears and also expose side and rear elevations of the end units.

In addition to the alleyways, some large areas today lie vacant and unused, symbolizing contemporary characteristics of neighborhood deterioration and resultant demolition. These vacant areas segment the continuous flow of architectural block faces.

Unit Considerations

The Otterbein rowhouse is generally designed as a narrow, 10-24' wide rectangular form with flat facades, minimally interrupted by stoops, entrance ways and area ways. Long narrow facade openings for windows and doors are typically arranged in strict gridlike rows. Entrances and accompanying stoops are set up above a low basement or placed at grade level. Ornamental architectural detailing is minimal. In the process of inventorying the Otterbein area, it was necessary to designate categories of unit types for the purpose of determining original architectural appointments and the origins of those designs. Research indicated two major groupings: Federal Row style, and Greek Revival style, with a few units of no particular style.

Although the units were generally built to reflect a particular building style, construction dates have varied and over time some modifications to the original design intent have been made. It is also apparent that although many of the units were faithful to the period style, they were often produced by builders who were interested in ease of construction and economy and not necessarily designed by architects. Consequently, some of the elements of decoration, particularly in the Federal Row structures, were sparingly used.

One purpose of this study is to point out the original design intent of the period style, as both a guide to their analysis and as a basis for rehabilitation and restoration.

Federal Row

The Federal period of architecture evolved after the Revolutionary War. The units began to appear in the Otterbein area in the early 1800's. The major design elements are aimed at simplicity and symmetry. Brick construction of a flat, planar facade with little ornamentation, is predominant.

Roof are pitched with single dormers on the center line of the front facade with double chimneys. The height varies from 2 to 2½ to 3 stories and windows are generally 6 over 6 style, double hung sash. Entranceways are simple doors of wood paneled construction with a three-light transom over the door.

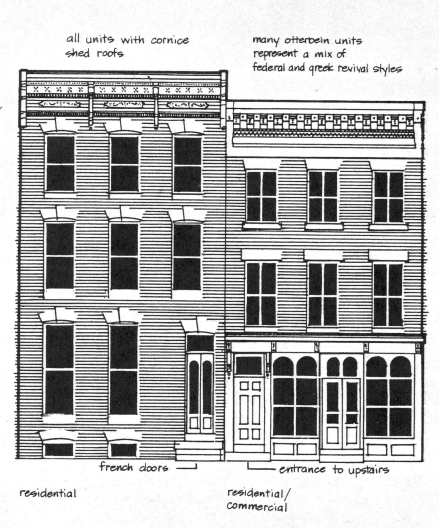

all units with cornice
shed roofs

many otterbein units
represent a mix of
federal and greek revival styles

french doors

entrance to upstairs

residential

residential/
commercial

Otterbein—Greek Revival Units

Design Elements

Although many of the units in Otterbein were designed along the principles of Greek Revival and Federal Row houses, it is important that each unit be viewed not only for its degree of successful interpretation of that period, but also for its original design intent. Certain design elements that should be understood and visually analyzed are facade treatment, proportions and rhythm. The facade as viewed from the street is an essential element in this visual analysis. The two story Federal Row units usually have a more visibile roof as well as the Greek Revival unit's conrice detail. However, the 2½ to 3 story unit's roof has less visual impact from the street. These factors should be taken into account when detailing the roof structure and front facade.

Entrance detailing, cornices and windows should complement each other in order to create a unified facade rather than a carnival of competing elements. The design elements should never appear as a series of elements with individual emphasis but as parts of a total design statement. For example, on 2½ and 3 story Federal Row units having a less visible roof and less impact, the design elements should be more restrained in order to create the proper design balance.

The proportions of the roof and wall area complement and balance each other. The window design and color in both flat facade and roof dormers tie together, and the brick, walls, and chimney are the same.

Greek Revival

The period of architecture refers to a time when architecture borrowed designs from classical monuments. In Otterbein the Greek Revival units have flat roofs with cornice detailing. The units are vertical in overall proportion and the design elements are vertical in emphasis. The units are generally 3 stories in height with more design articulation on lintels and sills and elaborately patterned cornice and entrance details. French doors and vestibule areas were a design feature of structures built later. Windows are double hung with 6 over 6 sash in early units and 2 over 2 in later units, with taller proportioned window openings. The elaborate cornice serves to visually terminate the building facade, much as the pitched roof terminates the Federal Row unit facade. The units with an elaborate cornice usually have ornate entrance detailing which tends to provide design balance.

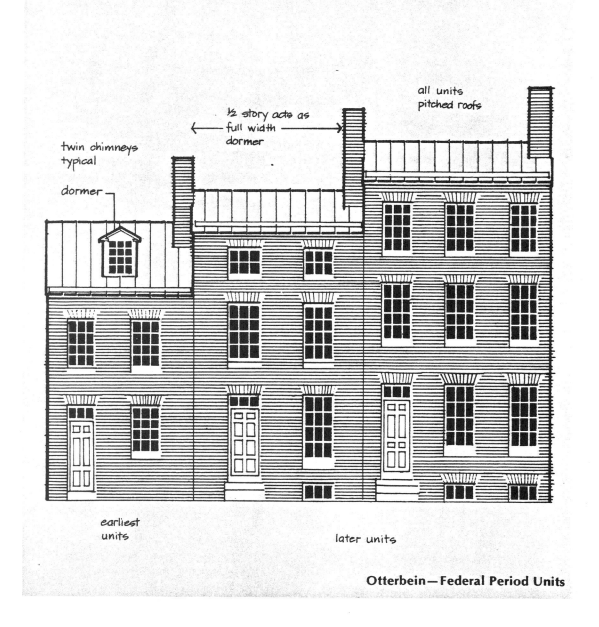

twin chimneys typical

dormer

½ story acts as full width dormer

all units pitched roofs

earliest units

later units

Otterbein—Federal Period Units

How to Make Cities Liveable

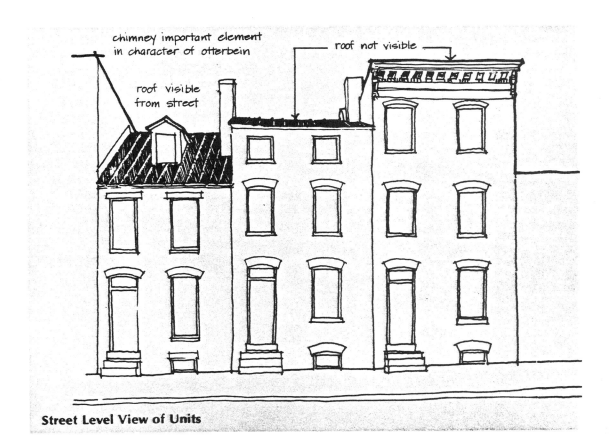

chimney important element in character of otterbein

roof not visible

roof visible from street

Street Level View of Units

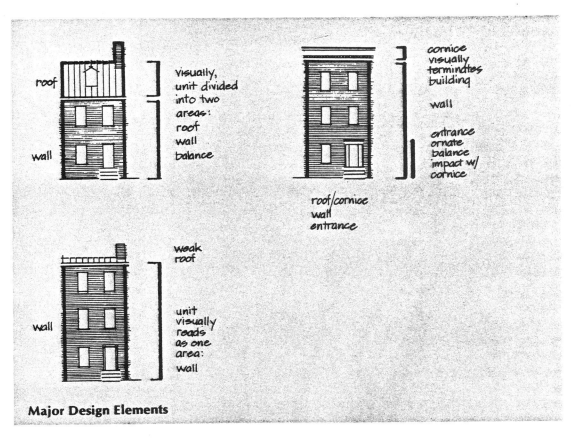

roof

wall

visually, unit divided into two areas: roof wall balance

cornice visually terminates building

wall

entrance ornate balance impact w/ cornice

roof/cornice wall entrance

weak roof

wall

unit visually reads as one area: wall

Major Design Elements

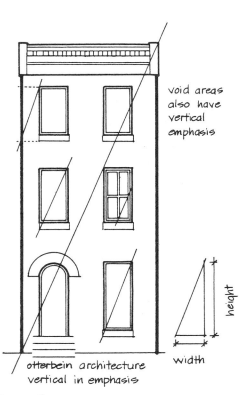

void areas also have vertical emphasis

height

width

otterbein architecture vertical in emphasis

Proportions

equal   variable

Rhythm

Summary Characteristics	**FEDERAL ROW**	**GREEK REVIVAL**
FACADE Three major areas that make up the facade are:		
ROOF AREAS	2 story units have the most visible roof from the street; 2½ and 3 story units, roof has less visual impact — 2 and 3 story units usually have dormers	Cornice is important; it visually terminates the building and functions as the roof element
ENTRANCE AREAS	Entrance has the same impact as the windows; it is not treated as a major statement	Some units have more emphasis placed on the entry area
WALL AREAS	2, 2½, and 3 story brick walls, basically flat, un-interrupted surfaces; all levels are treated the same	3 and 4 story brick walls, some lower levels are designed as storefront and treated differently than upper levels
PROPORTIONS — the relationship of height to width, includes the total building outline plus individual elements such as windows, entran-ces, etc.	Use of rectangular forms which are vertical in emphasis, tall in proportion	Generally taller in proportion than the Federal Row units
RHYTHM — refers to the regular occurence of elements such as doors, windows, etc.	More regular occurence of elements	Earlier units with regular occurence of elements, later units with more variation

How to Make Cities Liveable

Use of Color

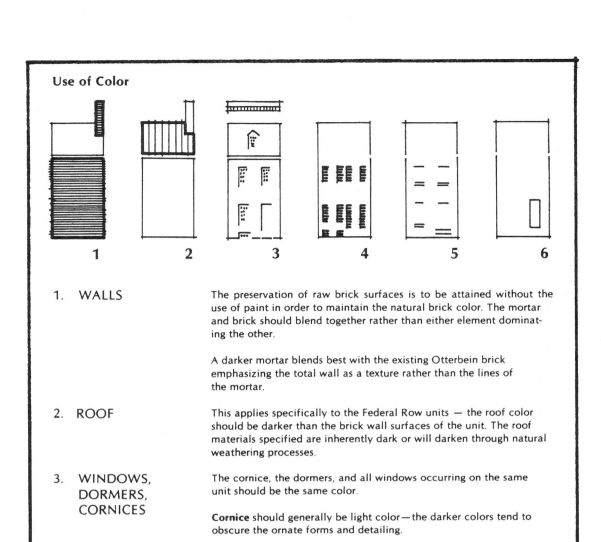

1   2   3   4   5   6

1. **WALLS**

The preservation of raw brick surfaces is to be attained without the use of paint in order to maintain the natural brick color. The mortar and brick should blend together rather than either element dominating the other.

A darker mortar blends best with the existing Otterbein brick emphasizing the total wall as a texture rather than the lines of the mortar.

2. **ROOF**

This applies specifically to the Federal Row units — the roof color should be darker than the brick wall surfaces of the unit. The roof materials specified are inherently dark or will darken through natural weathering processes.

3. **WINDOWS, DORMERS, CORNICES**

The cornice, the dormers, and all windows occurring on the same unit should be the same color.

Cornice should generally be light color — the darker colors tend to obscure the ornate forms and detailing.

Windows
a) Paint all parts a light shade.
b) Paint the window casing and frame dark with the moving parts or sash painted white.

4. **SHUTTERS**

All shutters on the same unit must be painted the same color. Traditionally they were painted darker colors.

5. **SILLS, LINTELS, ENTRY STOOPS**

Sills and Lintels
a) Wood — traditionally painted to imitate stone — should be painted grey or light tones.
b) Stone — should be repaired and if necessary painted to match the original color.
c) Brick — should be repaired to retain the raw brick surface.

Stoops may be painted to imitate natural colors such as stone.

6. **DOORS**

a) can be treated to be consistent with window elements — painted same color
b) if painted an optional color it should be compatible with other colors used on the unit.

7. **MISCELLANEOUS**

Miscellaneous items such as gutters, downspouts, vents, etc. should be painted to blend with their background surface — should not be emphasized by different color.

FACADE: Facades can be broken down into three major areas: the roof area comprising the dormers, chimneys, cornices; the entrance area including the stoop, doors; and the wall area including the brick texture and windows. The Federal Row unit has a roof area and wall area with the entrance having the same impact as the windows. The roof area and wall area complement and balance each other. The window design and color of first and second floors is the same as the window in the dormer also the brick used in the walls and the chimney is the same. In the Greek Revival units the cornice visually terminates the building. The entrance area is usually more ornately designed to complement the cornice.

PROPORTIONS: Proportion is the relationship of height to width. The use of the rectilinear forms, which are vertical in emphasis, is common to Otterbein. Windows, doors, and the building outlines are tall in proportion. The Greek Revival units tend to be taller in proportion than the Federal Row units. Roof areas and cornices are of horizontal emphasis and visually terminate the buildings. Any elements replaced or added to the unit should be of consistent proportions in order to produce a unified design.

RHYTHM: Rhythm refers to the regular occurrence of elements such as windows, doors, and the details of the cornice. In Federal Row units there is a regular occurrence of those elements or equal spacing of elements. In some of the Greek Revival units, unequal or altered spacing of elements was used as a design device. For example, varying window heights, space between windows and varying floor heights were often used to emphasize the verticality of a building.

DESIGN DETAILS: Many of the units, while sympathetic to period style, were built to produce homes that were simple and clean in construction. The emphasis was on flat, planar wall surfaces. The detailing came from pattern books and was applied to the building rather than integrated into it. The details were of better quality and craft than most produced today.

It is most important to study the facade of each unit to try to determine the original intent of the builder in order to determine the success of the design. This does not mean that the amount of trim applied to the surface necessarily generates a design of high quality nor does age imply excellent design. What might be old might also be an example of the mistakes that were made during that time. It should be emphasized that inappropriate detailing can markedly affect the appearance not only of the units but of the whole street.

MATERIAL: The original indigenous materials, e.g. brick, wood and glass used in Otterbein, were derived locally. Replacement of damaged or missing elements of material may be done through salvage or duplication.

COLOR: Color is a means of emphasis. Used wrongly or too intensely, it provides inappropriate emphasis to details. In this regard, the more intense chromatic colors tend to distract from a harmonious design and are discouraged. In general earth tones should be used. Lighter colors bring out elements from the building surfaces whereas darker colors tend to cause elements to recede. It is also recommended that semi-gloss paint be used because gloss reflects light and emphasizes defects.

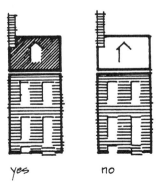

yes   no

roof traditionally dark in color

How to Make Cities Liveable

the use of color –
keep number of colors to min.
pastels & primary colors inappropriate
semi-gloss paint best finish

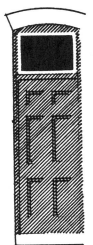

where a dark color
is used for trim,
paint moving parts
of window white

REPRODUCING AND DUPLICATING DETAILS: In instances where pieces of the facade or details are damaged or missing, the alternatives are restoration, duplication or replacement through salvage. Consideration must be given to the scale and proportion of those elements, whether their emphasis is strong or minimal, vertical or horizontal. For example, thin aluminum door or window details are inappropriate in relation to the proportion of other unit elements.

Smaller embellishments such as moldings and dentils are of secondary importance in relation to the overall unit design. For example, the overall proportions and mass of a cornice are more important than the amount of detailed dentil work it contains. Beware of details that are not of period style, are imitations or are nonfunctional in relation to the building.

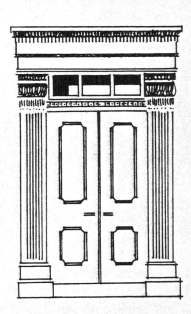

it is most important to reproduce the size and proportions of trim; details and flourishes are of secondary importance

Reproducing Trim

The foregoing material dealt with Architectural Considerations in the Otterbein summary report, the following deals with the same subject as contained in the Barre Circle summary report. There is a certain amount of overlap and duplication, but rather than deleting and editing, the following is presented as it was set forth in greater detail for the Barre Circle homesteaders. (Editor)

Image

The primary image of row housing is its block face. Few buildings are visually prominent either through flamboyance of style, irregularity of form or marked difference in materials. It is important to emphasize that each residential unit is part of a larger architectural facade. A sensitivity to the overall appearance of the block face is essential in renovating each unit, as a complementary part of the larger whole.

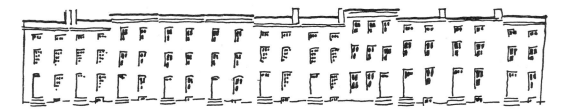

The architecture of **Barre Circle** is generally restrained and of pedestrian scale.

Elements

The ability to address the whole block as a single entity cannot be overstressed. The interrelationship of elements which when combined create the overall block character should be the primary concern when evaluating exterior modifications. A positive architectural facade cannot be accomplished by restrictive/mandatory statements but through understanding these relationships.

Architectural courtesy - The sensitivity of how one building can complement and be complemented by adjacent units.

The following will identify the major elements of the block facade:

Wall

The wall is a collection of united and aligned flat brick panels, 2 to 3 stories in height. Window and door openings provide the only interruption to this continuous surface. The roofscape and stoops give some definition and variation to the upper and lower edges of the wall.

Openings

Door and window openings form an attractive rhythm along the block face and have a strong impact on the architectural character. Generally window openings are similar in size, and rectangular in shape. Arched lintels appear on many units. A majority of openings align vertically and horizontally. This symmetrical arrangement should not be modified.

Roofscape

The roofscape is one area of renovation taken for granted, and modified with little concern for its effect on neighborhood appearance, the irregularities of pitched roofs and cornices give interest to the skyline, an obvious relief to the uninterrupted wall. The roofs and cornices also act as a visual terminus - capping off the building wall.

Stoops

Stoops and their maintenance have a special heritage in Baltimore. They long have been an expression of personal pride and neighborhood self-esteem. Esthetically stoops provide definition and emphasis to the entrance and a sculptural interruption to the wall and sidewalk surfaces.

Texture and function

Two other elements of the block facade would be texture and function. Texture is the arrangement, size and quantity of repeated items, for example, sills, lintels, and shutters. Consider the modification of existing or the introduction of new repeated elements. In function it is important to understand how the block face was originally oriented towards the street with private areas and service access to the block interior.

History

The typical Barre Circle row house ranges in size from 10-20 feet in width, 30-40 feet in depth and 2 to 3 stories in height. Many units have a partially buried basement with windows occurring at grade and ornamentation was minimal. Although the units were generally built to reflect a particular building style, construction dates varied and over time some modifications to the original design intent have been made.

Federal period

According to style and history, the units may be divided into two groups, Federal Row and Greek Revival. The major visual differences between styles, being in roof configuration and architectural appointments. The architecture is generally of a harmonious, pleasing design. Both styles reflect a builder's rationalism in ease of construction and economy of materials using readily available materials, such as brick, wood and stone. Minimal detailing was applied (stuck on) rather than being made integral with the architecture, and came from pattern books available at the time. Few buildings were visually prominent over their neighbors.

THE FEDERAL PERIOD STYLE WAS DEVELOPED SHORTLY AFTER THE REVOLUTIONARY WAR. BARRE CIRCLE UNITS OCCURRING ABOUT 1820-1840.

MAJOR CHARACTERISTICS

- pitched roof
- brick construction, flat planar facade
- original windows 6 over 6 double-hung
- brick sills & lintels
- simplicity & symmetry few architectural appointments
- original doors - wood panel construction

brick chimney

½ window represents full width dormer

3 light transom original

TYPICAL FEDERAL PERIOD

How to Make Cities Liveable

Architectural Considerations

Greek Revival

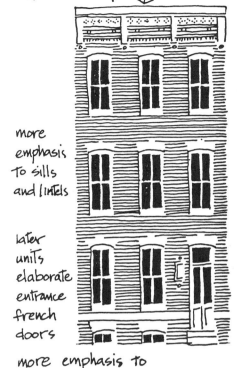

entablature - visually capped building

more emphasis to sills and lintels

later units elaborate entrance french doors

more emphasis to vertical proportions

GREEK REVIVAL REFERS TO THE PERIOD IN WHICH ARCHITECTURE WAS INFLUENCED BY CLASICAL MONUMENTS. BUILT AFTER 1840

MAJOR CHARACTERISTICS

- all units have shed roof which are not visible from the street

- units originally had entablature (cornice)

- brick construction - flat planar facade

- windows originally 6 over 6 early. 2 over 2 later double hung wood.

- increased emphasis to sills and lintels

The process of architectural evaluation will fall into two parts, identification and appraisal. Identification meaning the ability to recognize the visual elements which make up the Barre Circle row housing architecture. Appraisal being the skill to examine and assign values to these visual elements.

- **Design**
- **Material**
- **Color**

Appraisal should be concerned with achieving a desired neighborhood image by judging the impact of architectural modifications to this image. One system for appraisal - visual analysis - would be to look at - Design - Material - Color

Although many of the units in Barre Circle were designed along the principles of Greek Revival and Federal period architecture, it is important that each unit be viewed not only for its degree of successful interpretation of that period, but also for its original functional intent.

Federal period had simple, economic, functional solutions.

small window panes
brick lintels
no decoration

Any elements added should be functional beauty in sparseness.

Typical Federal Design

Greek Revival beginning to show decoration fashion concern

taller proportions decoration, entrance sill, lintel, cornice.

Any element added should reflect period.

Typical Greek Revival Design

Design

Detailing of entrances, cornices, windows, etc. should complement each other in order to create a unified facade rather than a carnival of competing elements. The design elements should never appear as a group of unrelated elements, but as a total unit.

Design will be referred to in general terms as the size, location and arrangement of the elements which make up the building. The following will take into consideration the original configuration and the impact of altering it.

Facade

Facades can be broken down into three areas: roofs, which include the cornice(because of its visual function of capping the front facade), entrance area(including the stoop and hardware), and wall area(including brick and windows).

Federal period

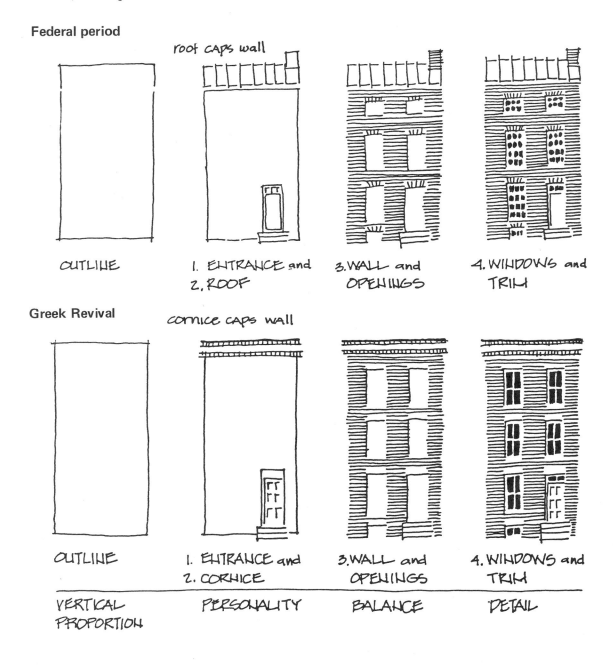

Greek Revival

Proportions

Proportions will be discussed as the relationship of height to width. In Barre Circle the use of rectilinear forms and openings which are vertical in emphasis, is predominant. Windows, doors and the building outline are tall in proportion. Generally the Greek Revival units tend to be taller in proportion than the Federal units. Roof areas and cornices are horizontal in emphasis and visually terminate the building. Introduction of elements of less than tall proportions produce confusing contradicting impressions. This should be considered when working with the side and rear of the units.

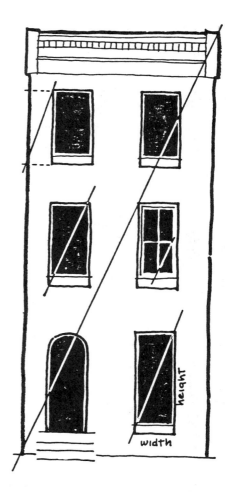

Rhythm

Rhythm refers to the regular occurrence of elements such as windows and doors. In Federal period units there is an equal spacing of elements. In some Greek Revival units unequal or progressive spacing was used as a design device. For example, varying window heights and spaces between windows was used to emphasize the verticality of a building. Some units in Barre Circle may have elements which have been relocated or altered at a later date which were located off center or unbalanced in appearance.

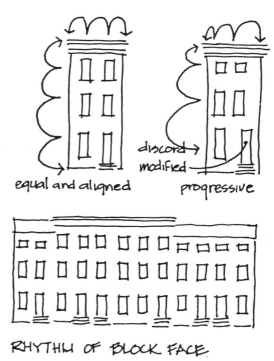

equal and aligned   progressive

discord modified

RHYTHM OF BLOCK FACE

NO   YES

The amount of trim applied to the surface does not imply quality, nor does age determine excellent design. A wagon wheel would be out of place on the front facade as would the application of carpenter gothic designs which occurred toward the end of the 19th century. It should be emphasized that inappropriate detailing can markedly affect the appearance of the unit and the whole block.

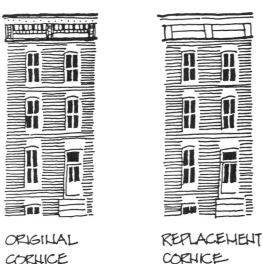

ORIGINAL   REPLACEMENT
CORNICE   CORNICE

In instances where pieces of facade or details are damaged or missing, the alternatives are restoration, renovation or replacement either from salvaged sources or procured new. Of prime importance is the scale and proportions of items, tiny details and moldings are of less importance in relation to overall design. For example, the overall proportions and mass of a cornice is more important that the amount of detailed dentil work it contains.

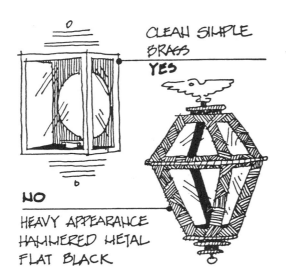

CLEAN SIMPLE BRASS
YES

NO
HEAVY APPEARANCE
HAMMERED METAL
FLAT BLACK

Beware of details that are not of period style, either Federal or Greek Revival. Also beware of imitation or "phony colony" items. If period style is unavailable, use an item of simple, straight forward design.

Appropriate materials

The original indigenous materials, e.g. brick, wood and stone used in Barre Circle were derived locally. Replacement of damaged or missing elements may be done through salvage or duplication. It is encouraged in renovation that materials identical to the original be used. Contemporary synthetic materials, e.g., plastic and aluminum, have a different character, appearance, quality, when compared to the original elements. An aluminum door does not give the same impression as an oak paneled door - sound, color, weight, texture, maintenance, insulation and longevity.

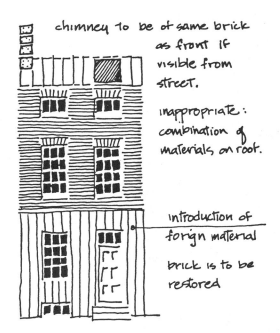

chimney to be of same brick as front if visible from street.

inappropriate: combination of materials on roof.

introduction of forign material

brick is to be restored

INAPPROPRIATE USE OF MATERIALS

Alternative materials

If the duplication or replacement of materials is difficult because of economics or availability, then try to make the substitute as inconspicuous as possible, for example, painting an aluminum downspout a dark color to blend into background and give the appearance of heavy metal or coloring concrete to appear as stone.

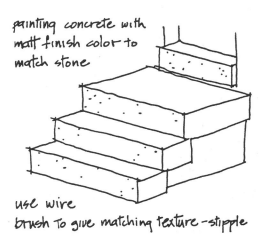

painting concrete with matt finish color to match stone

use wire brush to give matching texture - stipple

Formstone

Because of the predominance and visual importance of brick in Barre Circle a separate section will be devoted to the subject. Of importance here is the standard that brick on front facades will be restored. Replacement bricks may be found in local demolitions so as to match size and color.

units with formstone appear superficial out of place. care should be taken to restore to original brick.

INAPPROPRIATE - FORMSTONE

Cornices

The cornice may be described as a large molding strip running horizontally along the upper leading edge of the front facade. Its use and design were borrowed from the entablature of classical architecture. The cornice provides a strong visual terminus to the street facade roofscape and its proper renovation will have a strong and positive impression on the street image.

Repair

STERILE FACADE WITHOUT CORNICE

THE CORNICE VISUALLY CAPS THE ARCHITECTURE.

Unless repair is completely unfeasible all cornices should be preserved and repaired.

On units where the cornice has previously been removed a new one should be fabricated utilizing designs from similar architecture in the area.

Replacement

THE INTRICACY OF DETAILS IS LEAST IMPORTANT

In those instances of cornice replacement, care should be taken to achieve correct proportions and massing. Detailing is of lesser importance.

Color of cornices should match window colors.

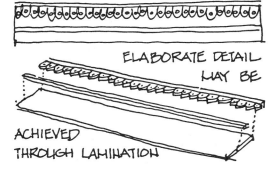

ELABORATE DETAIL MAY BE

ACHIEVED THROUGH LAMINATION

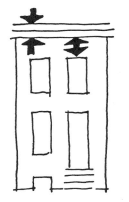

Consider the size, shape and location of the cornice by observing restored units of similar design.

How to Make Cities Liveable

Guidelines for Exterior Restoration

Although changes for modern residential use are necessary, the architectural character of Otterbein can be maintained and enhanced if a careful and sensitive restoration program is followed. In order to achieve a sensitive restoration, an awareness of basic design principles and how to apply them is essential. This awareness can guide each resident's individual restoration effort in creating a unity, both in appearance and value for the Otterbein project. Traditional building forms and materials must be respected. Also characteristic features including proportional relationships, facade compositions and textural qualities should be maintained or sensitively restored.

Within the guidelines the emphasis will be to offer as many options as possible in reference to the framework of the restoration and rehabilitation principles. It is recognized that contemporary considerations such as the implications of heating and cooling and availability of craft skills as well as economic choices, must be taken into account.

All plans for new construction, demolition, exterior rehabilitation and repair of existing buildings, as well as all proposals concerning the erection of signs, awnings or other features in the Otterbein district, must be submitted to the Architectural Review Committee of the Otterbein Homestead Area for their review and consideration as they relate to these guidelines.

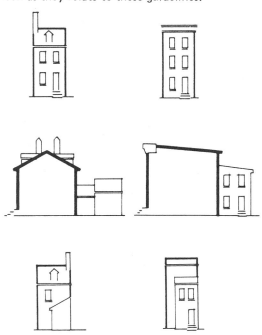

Format

The format in each of the following sections of the guidelines is a stated design objective, second, a list of the minimal standards prepared by the consultants and approved by the residents and ; third a range of considerations that support those standards providing descriptive techniques and alternatives in obtaining them. The various sections of the guidelines are as follows:

FRONT FACADE: Because of the visual importance of the front facade this section will have the most specific guidelines. In this area the greatest emphasis should be placed on the original design intent of the unit.

SIDE FACADE: The side facades are of two types: street corner units which normally have a second front facade and should be treated as such, and the sides which appear within interiors of the block along the alleyways. For these units alternatives will be provided which compromise the original design intent with contemporary needs as an area of transition.

REAR FACADE: In the rear areas the concern will be with design solutions that allow for contemporary living circumstances in harmony with the neighborhood.

WALLS/BRICK: This section deals with restoring and preserving the original brick wall surfaces that exemplify the character of Otterbein.

WINDOWS: The vertically proportioned windows of the Otterbein units must be sensitively restored in order to achieve the historic architectural style.

ROOF AREAS: Both the Federal Row pitched roofs and the Greek Revival flat roofs should be treated in a manner that preserves the original skyline and design characteristics.

ENTRANCES: Doors and entrances, especially those on the front facade, should be maintained and repaired with considerable care.

CONVENIENCES: The contemporary conveniences such as antennas, air conditioning units, vents, trash storage facilities, should be designed and located to minimize the impact on the building design and neighborhood image.

Objective

The traditional character of Barre Circle can be revived and enhanced through a careful and sensitive renovation program. The following text and illustrations will first identify the original architectural features and functions, secondly they will consider residential objectives to determine if renovation or modification is necessary and, thirdly the following sections will look at the impact of this implementation on the building esthetics and neighborhood image.

Front Facade: Because of the visual importance, this section will have the most specific guidelines. The greatest emphasis should be placed on original design intent.

Side Facade: Are of two types, street corner facades which because of neighborhood impact are treated as a front facade. Interior block side facades, which allow modification for contemporary needs.

Rear Facade: Concern for contemporary living in harmony with the neighborhood.

Roof Area: Preserve the original skyline character.

Wall/brick: Restore and preserve original surfaces.

Entrance: Door, stoop, hardware. Develop personal expression through traditional design.

Windows: Concern for personal expression, traditional design, and contemporary function.

Hardware: Modern convenience with minimum visual impact.

Site: Contemporary outdoor living within an urban area - improve the micro-climate.

**Front
Side
Rear
Site**

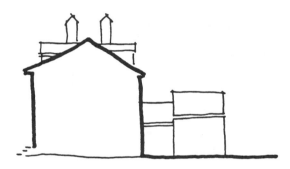

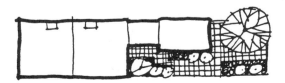

Front facade

Objective: To restore the front facade based on the original design
intentions of the unit.

STANDARDS:

1. Brick work to be repaired, cleaned and repointed to its original
   character, and existing window, door and alleyway openings shall be
   retained or restored to period size and proportion.

2. Original architectural appointments, including but not limited to
   lintels, sills, fascias, cornices, and eaves, shall be restored and duplicated
   to period style.

3. Front facades of adjoining houses of similar architectural style
   shall be restored to a uniform character and complementary color
   of roof materials, window styles, and shutter treatments.

4. Existing dormers and chimneys on the fronts are to be retained
   and to be repaired.

5. Original roof pitches are to be retained.

6. Period storefronts may be retained or restored to proportions of
   period residential style.

The front facade is the street image to the neighborhood and the formal entrance of the unit. Historically, it was given the most design consideration and was often constructed with higher quality brick and better quality windows. The facades of those units facing on alleyways, such as Welcome Alley, are also to be considered front facades.

As a part of the front facade, the roof areas, dormers, and chimneys visible from the street must be preserved and the shape of the building facade unaltered.

Design elements to be restored or added to the front facades must be done so with great care in order to maintain the original design intent. Because of the simplicity of the proportions, relationship of massing and a minimum amount of appointments, the addition of any architectural feature which might detract or interrupt the planar quality of the front facade is discouraged. Certain features such as bay windows, porches, porticos, and wrought iron catwalks that protrude from a front facade are particularly inappropriate. Furthermore, elements of other design periods or elements of the correct architectural period but not characteristic of Baltimore will be discouraged. As an example, wrought iron steps are correct for Federal and Greek Revival period, but were not used extensively in Baltimore.

In instances where design elements are out of proportion or inconsistent, care should be taken in correcting the inconsistencies. Door and window openings may be realigned, incongruous sills or lintels may be modified to an appropriate example.

Reconstruction of missing or destroyed elements should be undertaken with the use of salvage materials or new materials which respect the original proportions, massing and texture. Intricate and expensively reproduced details are not necessary as long as their replacements are compatible in scale and reflective of the period.

Federal Row

The main distinguishing features of the brick fronts are simple design, a minimum of embellishments, a pitched roof with dormers and chimneys.

The front brick is usually of better quality, although some of the earlier units employed a softer, more porous brick. Care should be taken in cleaning and repointing older surfaces and in matching brick size and color.

Window, door and alleyway openings should be retained unless they differ from the original design intent. Openings that have been sealed off or were integral elements of the original design may be reopened. Area ways, open or closed should be the option of the owner.

Sills and lintels should be restored or duplicated. Units without restorable sills or lintels may copy the style from a similar period. Original roof pitches must be maintained in the front and owners are encouraged to retain the rear portion as well.

Greek Revival

Distinguishing features of these units are the vertically proportioned front elevation, the vertical windows and doors, and the horizontal cornice.

In most cases, front facade bricks are of better quality than those used on the sides, due to the stronger emphasis on frontal appearance.

Incompatible window and door alignments may be altered and the area ways may be sealed and restored. Sills and lintels are usually more elaborate but should not be difficult or costly to restore or duplicate. An alternative is the introduction of new lintels and sills characteristic of the period, but less complex in nature. For example, soldier courses of brick with back-up steel angles are a replacement for damaged, ornate stone or wood.

Actual roof materials are not of major concern as the flat roofs are not visible from the street. The cornice, however, serves as the upper terminus of the unit and should be carefully considered. Cornice treatment on corner units must be especially considered and designed in terms of continuity around the corner in the appropriate alignment.

Multiplex

Multiplex refers to those units, although individual in plan, that are attached in groups of 2,3 or 4 and form a common front facade. In such cases, the major design elements must be restored in a uniform manner. The elements of the facade that must be restored in common material and color are the brick surface, the roof surface, gutters and downspouts, the use of snowguards and window treatment.

The elements of the facade that will allow individual expression are entrance ways and doors and shutters, with individual but compatible colors.

Non-conforming structures

Those units which did not represent the period style and do not fit into the two major unit categories should conform at least to those guidelines that are applicable. For example, guidelines for brick preservation, roofs, windows, entrances and contemporary conveniences should be followed.

In the instance of non-conforming structures, the element of architectural courtesy takes on added significance. This necessitates respect for the adjoining units in material, color and proportions.

In some instances, front openings have been historically used that are out of character with the original period style. As an example is the use of a large, arched window on the first floor which is not aligned with those openings above. It was the tradition in many Baltimore neighborhoods that those openings be used to allow for the passage of caskets in family funeral ceremonies. Such openings, although contrary to period style, may be retained.

Front facade guidelines

dormers and chimneys on front to be repaired

brick work to be restored

original roof pitch on federal units to be restored

lintels, sills, fascia, eaves to be restored or duplicated

original window, door and alleyway openings to be retained

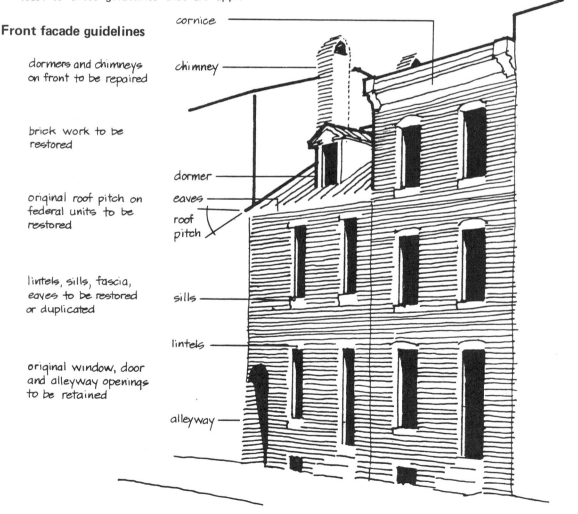

cornice

chimney

dormer

eaves

roof pitch

sills

lintels

alleyway

Non-Period rehabilitation

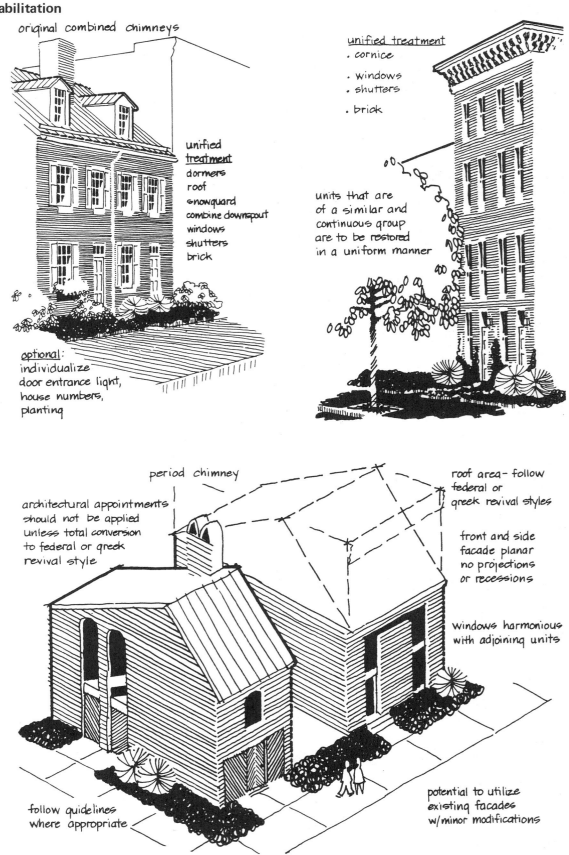

original combined chimneys

unified
treatment
dormers
roof
snowguard
combine downspout
windows
shutters
brick

optional:
individualize
door entrance light,
house numbers,
planting

unified treatment
. cornice
. windows
. shutters
. brick

units that are
of a similar and
continuous group
are to be restored
in a uniform manner

period chimney

architectural appointments
should not be applied
unless total conversion
to federal or greek
revival style

roof area- follow
federal or
greek revival styles

front and side
facade planar
no projections
or recessions

windows harmonious
with adjoining units

follow guidelines
where appropriate

potential to utilize
existing facades
w/minor modifications

Miscellaneous

period storefronts may be
restored or modified to
residential character

coal chutes and basement
entrances and areaways may
be retained or covered.
retention offers pleasant
clutter to pedestrian area.

alleyways should be
lighted and secured with
a gate; wrought iron is
preferred — allows view
down alley and air
movement in summer

Scattered throughout the Otterbein area are some examples of wood commercial fronts of period style. These fronts are often of pleasing proportions and simple in design with the majority of their wood structures intact. Such store fronts are of period style, are reflective of historic commercial uses, and may be retained.

The original and period commercial front buildings undoubtedly provided the owner with living quarters above and, as such, now offer an opportunity for commercial use. Even though the majority of these units have been offered as residences, it is not necessary to replace the commercial front character. Owners are encouraged to respect the existing commercial "openness" and through interior devices such as shutters and blinds, adapt them to residential use. In those instances where it is impractical or undesirable to restore the commercial fronts, they may be replaced with residential scale windows and door openings that are compatible and line up with the existing upper story windows.

There are also a few residential units in Otterbein that in more recent years were converted for commercial use. These unfortunately, have been converted in inappropriate ways and in poor taste. It is recommended in these cases that the storefronts be eliminated and the lower levels be restored to their original residential character.

Objective

The most critical portions of the guidelines for the Barre Circle area apply to the front facades. Historically, the building fronts were given the most design considerations and often constructed with better quality materials. The front facade comprises a major portion of the street image and represents the formal public image of the architecture. The objective of the following is to illustrate how to preserve and enhance the architecture's original character.

Design

Because of the original design simplicity and the minimal use of architectural appointments, these units are particularly sensitive to the addition of any elements which are out of character. Any interruption to the planar quality of the front facade is discouraged. Features such as bay windows, porches, porticos, and wrought iron catwalks that protrude from a front facade are particularly inappropriate. Furthermore, elements of another design period or items of the correct architectural period but not characteristic of Baltimore should be discouraged. As an example, wrought iron steps are correct for Federal and Greek Revival periods, but were not used extensively in Baltimore, so would be inappropriate in the Barre Circle row house redevelopment or restoration.

Existing modifications

In instances where design elements are inconsistent or modified from the original intent, the owner has the option to either preserve or correct incongruities after first getting permission from the architectural committee. For example, doors and window openings may be realigned, inappropriate sills or lintels may be modified to a suitable type or sealed openings may be reopened.

Sealed windows should be reopened

Inappropriate sills and lintels may be replaced

Modified or relocated window openings may be corrected

Replacement

Reconstruction of missing or destroyed items should be undertaken with the use of salvage materials which respect the original proportions, massing and texture. Intricate and expensively reproduced details are not necessary, as long as their replacements are compatible in scale and reflective of the period.

Symmetrical units

Symmetrical units refer to an architectural group of repeated identical front facades. The repeated arrangement of duplicate windows, doors, cornices, eaves and brickwork. The object is to utilize this repetitive character to the advantage of the residents and neighborhood. To compete with, or deny the symmetry produces a mediocre collection of facades and does not take advantage of the architectural potential. Variation and individual expression can be provided within this repetitive architectural arrangement.

Group treatment

Save costs with combined purchases.

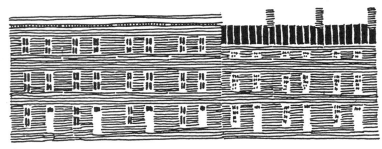

Items to be handled as a group.

Roof, cornice, eaves, brick, window and door frame, downspout and gutter.

Individual treatment

Pedestrian level - Area of individual treatment.

Items of individual treatment

Shutters and blinds, doors, stoops, landscaping, hardware and what shows through the windows.

Design

Symmetrical units can be compared with attending a formal dinner, with the men all wearing suits or tails. At first, all appear similar, then items of jewelry, ties, shoes or how the clothes fit become noticeable indicating personal preferences. Ignoring or cosmetically changing the symmetry is superficial and contradictory. This would be similar to the suited men wearing funny hats, brightly colored gloves or lipstick or if they were to be barefoot.

Wall/brick

Original location and pitch of the roof visible from the street is to be preserved.

Roof

Chimneys visible from the street should be repaired and pointed to match the front wall.

Downspouts and other hardware should be inconspicuous.

Entrance

Brickwork should be restored or repaired to match the original block and front facade.

Cornice

Sills and lintels should be restored.

Shutters and blinds are optional but, if used should match the original or those on adjacent units.

Windows

Original window and door openings to be preserved in the the original form or manner.

Retention of basement windows and areaways is optional.

Hardware

Hardware for house lights, handrails, mail boxes, burglar bars and other elements should be compatible and appropriate.

Site

Stoops should be restored in a traditional manner.

Alleyways should be retained with gates optional.

Cornices and eaves to be retained, and repaired or replaced.

Front planting should be appropriate and compatible with that on other units and in the neighborhood.

Side facade

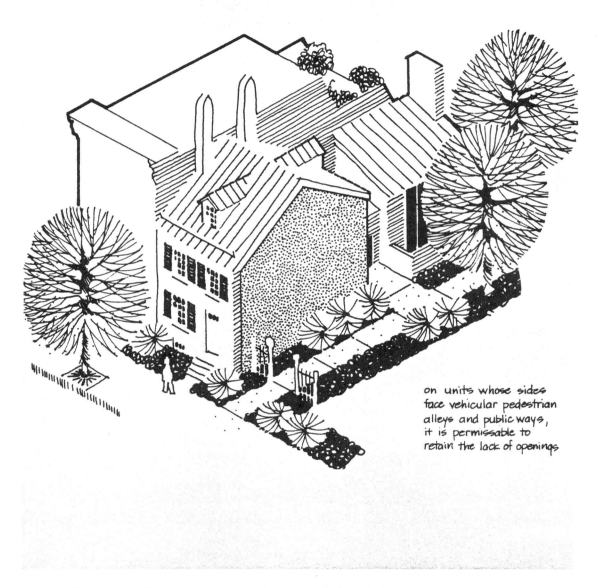

on units whose sides
face vehicular pedestrian
alleys and public ways,
it is permissable to
retain the lack of openings

Objective: On street-corner units, the side facade is considered as a
front facade.

STANDARDS:

1. Corner units that face two streets may retain existing compatible
openings or introduce new openings that are consistent with the
existing front or entrance facade.

2. On units facing vehicular-pedestrian alleys, or public ways, it is
permissible to retain existing openings or lack of openings: or to
provide new openings that are compatible with existing front openings.

How to Make Cities Liveable

Street Corner Units

The majority of side walls in rowhousing are common walls, and consequently have no visibility or facade. However, due to the nature of a grid street system, a block face is occasionally punctured by a narrow alleyway or a demolished unit, therefore many side facades do exist. It consequently becomes essential that these facades be given the proper consideration in the overall approach to the unit's restoration and rehabilitation.

The side facades are broken into two groups, street corner units which face onto street intersections and interior block units which face internal pedestrian or vehicular alleyways.

In the case where the side facade becomes a major facade to the street, it should be treated as a front facade with the appropriate guidelines applied. Corner units take on added significance in that they become entrance ways to the linear character of the neighborhood street. It is important to "turn the corner" with the design treatment so that the front entrance facade will not appear as only a veneer over a buildng of lesser quality.

The side facade of street corner units should be treated with the same considerations which relate to the original design intent of the unit. The side facade should be consistent in design, materials and color with the entrance front and harmonious with the adjoining facades. Intrusion of elements on the planar character of the walls, such as balconies, bay windows or wrought iron catwalks, are just as inappropriate here as on the front facade.

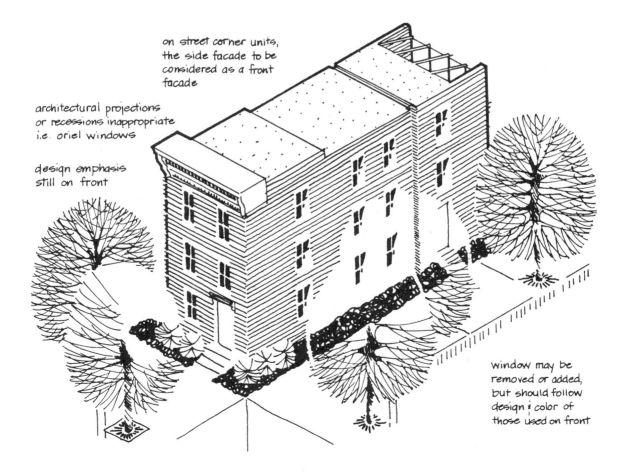

on street corner units, the side facade to be considered as a front facade

architectural projections or recessions inappropriate i.e. oriel windows

design emphasis still on front

window may be removed or added, but should follow design & color of those used on front

Openings that are compatible with those on the front may be introduced on the side facade of either street corner or interior block units.

Interior Block Units

Units whose sides face on the pededstrian or vehicular alleyways offer more flexibility in treatment than do the street corner units, since the visual impact is as a transition zone if more contemporary or functional alterations are being considered. It should be treated, however, as a facade compatible with the front if a more traditional appearance is desired.

A further consideration for the side facade is the quality of the existing surface material. Often the side facade materials were of a lesser quality and appearance due to the emphasis placed on the original front facade. Lesser quality materials might also exist on a side facade due to the elimination of an adjacent unit.

The existing surface materials are either brick or stucco. If feasible, the side facade should be restored to its original brick surface. However, if not appropriate, stucco may be repaired and then should be painted a color compatible with the brick on the front facade. It is generally desirable that the brick material of the front facade wrap around the corner of the side, thus providing the proper transitions of brick to stucco.

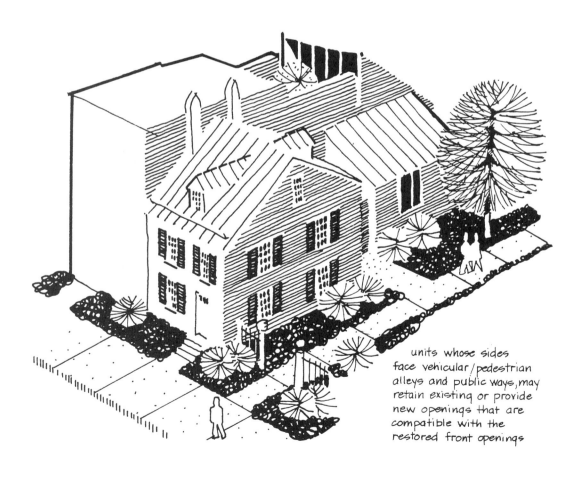

units whose sides face vehicular/pedestrian alleys and public ways, may retain existing or provide new openings that are compatible with the restored front openings

Street Corner Unit

RESIDENTS SHOULD TRY TO REDUCE FRONT FACADE AS VENEER IMAGE.

The following deals with end units with visible side facades. These facades may be divided into two groups. First, street corner units which face on to street intersections and have a strong visual impact on the neighborhood image. Second, having only a local visual impact, end units which face on to interior block situations.

- installation of windows on side facade is optional,
- considerations: windows should be the same size, design and color as those of the front. They should align horizontally and vertically and be of a symmetrical arrangement.

- rear building is considered the rear facade and may reflect more severe modifications.

- on Greek Revival units the cornice would not continue around the side,

- existing brick on the side facade may differ from that used on the front, but should be restored.

facia trim

Screen optional

Street corner units should continue the character of the front facade on to the side facade.

Interior Block Units

End units which face on to interiors have less visual impact upon neighborhood image and thus have more flexibility in exterior design solutions. They should be treated as a transition between the traditional front facade, and the potential alternatives of the rear.

Stucco

- often the side facade brick is of a poorer quality, the emphasis placed on the more exposed front facade. If brick is not restorable, stucco is appropriate if painted a light color such as cream or beige.

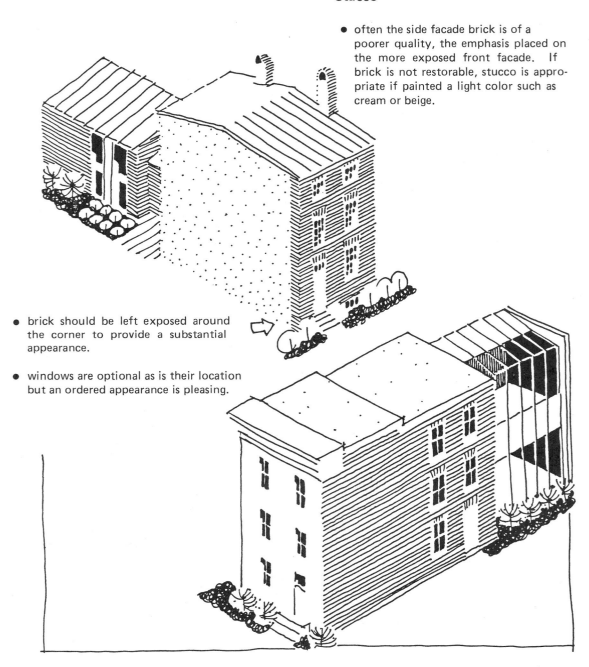

- brick should be left exposed around the corner to provide a substantial appearance.

- windows are optional as is their location but an ordered appearance is pleasing.

The original window openings on the front facade and street corner side facades shall be retained.

Wood or vinyl-clad wood construction, exterior storm windows and screens shall be permitted on all facades.

The choice of window design for the rear facades is up to the owner's discrimination. Some considerations to be evaluated are; improved light sources, solar orientation, insulation qualities, views and vistas.

Shutters and blinds are optional. If they are installed, a painted wood constructed design is required.

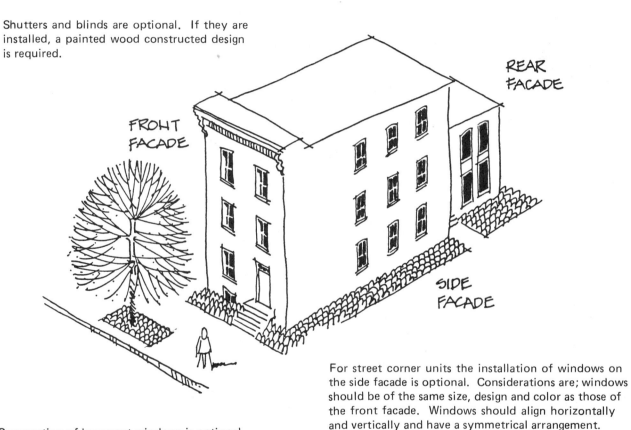

FRONT FACADE

REAR FACADE

SIDE FACADE

Preservation of basement windows is optional.

For street corner units the installation of windows on the side facade is optional. Considerations are; windows should be of the same size, design and color as those of the front facade. Windows should align horizontally and vertically and have a symmetrical arrangement.

All windows on front and side facades should be of the same color.

All major front facade windows should be of one design. Minor windows - basement, ½ etc., should be compatible with the major windows.

Rear facade

Objective: To present alternatives and considerations for the restoration, alteration or additions to the rear facade.

STANDARD:

1. Existing additions may be retained or removed.

2. New additions or alterations shall be compatible with existing structure and rear facade in both material and scale, and shall provide a transition between original structure and new additions.

3. New additions or alterations shall not intrude upon adjacent units' internal light source.

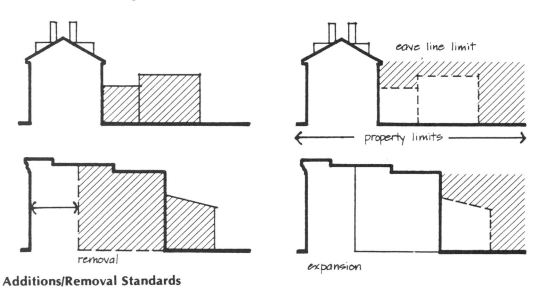

Additions/Removal Standards

Architectural Courtesy

The rear facade of the building offers the most opportunities for change and thus has the least limiting standards. The intent of these guidelines is to deal with existing or proposed alterations or additions that occur from the rear face of the original building to the rear yard property lines.

The original part of most of the residential units in Otterbein is generally easy to distinguish from the subsequent additions to that structure. The existing additions have historical precedent but do not necessarily conform to contemporary living standards and owners have the option of retaining the additions or modifying or removing them. Whatever alterations are proposed, they should relate to the original structure, be harmonious with the other units and not intrude on the functioning of adajacent units. Owners should be sensitive to the plans for adjacent units and are encouraged to coordinate their planning efforts with their neighbors.

The most common approach to rear facade alterations will probably be to accept the existing additions, repair or modify them, and remove any dilapidated elements. That is, however, but one approach. Another approach might be to totally remove all additions in a pure restoration of the original structure. This may create more options for the use of the rear yard area for both new structures or outdoor living spaces.

The rear facade additions and rear yards should be of three dimensional concern. The options are many but the planning should take into account the following:
1. the orientation of the rear portion as to sun and climate;
2. the need for additional light sources;
3. the potential use of any outdoor space as a garden or patio;
4. the unit's relationship to the rear pedestrian walkway;
5. surface accessibility to the rear;
6. location of air conditioning units, outdoor storage or work areas;
7. potential studio areas attached or detached;
8. any proposed change as it relates to adjacent units.

Removal

The concept of removing additions that have been added over time can allow for adaptation to a more contemporary living style. The reduction of house square footage will allow more exterior yard space for outdoor living, gardening, etc. and will also lessen heating and cooling loads.

One must remember that the more traditional living style was internal, whereas today more emphasis is placed on the use of adjacent or private outdoor spaces.

Additions

New additions or replacements of old ones should be compatible with the original structure, but do not necessarily have to repeat the original materials. New additions to the rear facade have the option of containing more contemporary window openings, such as sliding glass doors.

Additions should complement older structures, not dominate them. Even the more contemporary features should follow the scale and rhythm in massing of the original buildings. Materials that are indigenous to the area such as brick and stucco should be used. Materials such as stone, aluminum siding or plywood will not be acceptable. Roofing materials for new additions should comply with the acceptable roof materials as outlined in that section.

In cases where materials are removed from additions, they should be salvaged for use in new structures, in fences, or in outdoor landscape features.

Openings

Larger openings or more contemporary glazing is acceptable provided it is proportional, in harmony, and in scale.

Colors

Colors may vary from original structure but should be compatible.

Alterations

Alterations should take into account the exposure characteristics of the rear yards. Skylights may be added to provide more internal light. Roofs may be altered to create more usable space. Walls may be punctured to create more openness to the outdoor space or to generate new light sources.

Expansion and Removal Limits

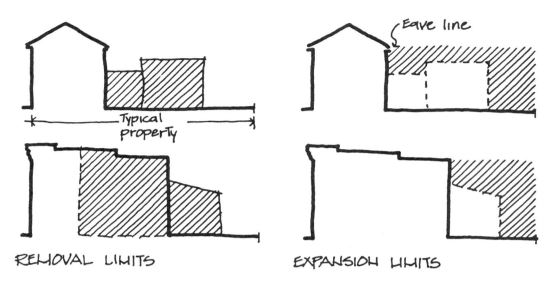

Cross section showing recommended limits of removal and expansion relative to the architectural style of the existing unit.

Ideas

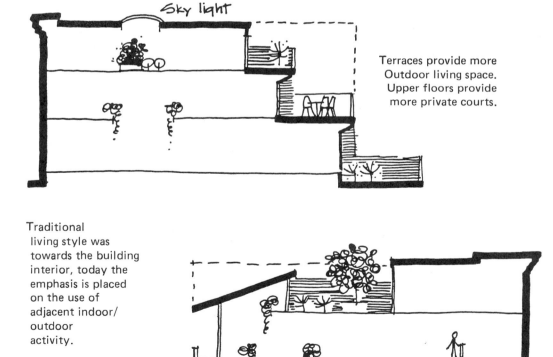

Terraces provide more Outdoor living space. Upper floors provide more private courts.

Traditional living style was towards the building interior, today the emphasis is placed on the use of adjacent indoor/outdoor activity.

Cross sections suggesting interior and exterior space modifications. Structural engineers should be consulted when owners consider major building changes.

Design

New rear additions and modifications should be compatible with the traditional street theme of the front. This does not suggest a repitition of the front facade architecture. Designs which are clean, simple and functional and of a modern attitude would be attractive. Proportions, rhythms, and massing of a similar scale to the front is also an important concern.

New roof pitches and skyline should be compatible with the existing building

Additions should complement older structures, not dominate them.

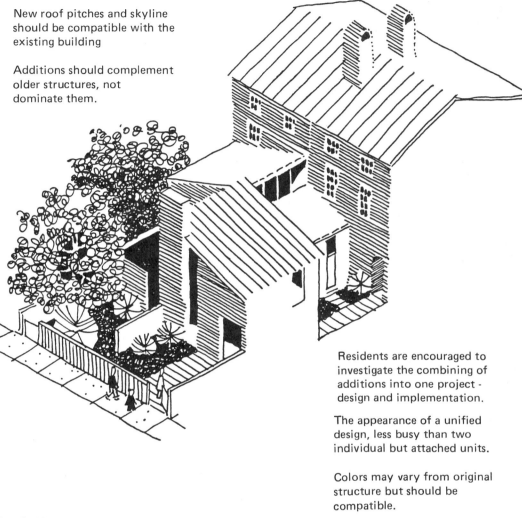

Residents are encouraged to investigate the combining of additions into one project - design and implementation.

The appearance of a unified design, less busy than two individual but attached units.

Colors may vary from original structure but should be compatible.

Concerns

The building rear and rear court should represent a multi-concern design process. Listed below are a few considerations in the planning and design of rear facades and rear yards in Barre Circle.

Environment - orientation to the sun: morning, noon and afternoon
      air movement
      prevailing breezes
      acoustics.
Views and vistas to preserve

Rear access - pedestrian and service

City codes

Location of building hardware, i.e. air conditioners, storage, etc.

Potential future buildng expansion.

Materials

Materials which are indigenous to Baltimore are recommended for construction of rear additions - brick, wood, stone are most appropriate. Architectural appointments and materials may be found through salvage. No alterations or additions will be permitted that intrude on the interior light source of an adjacent unit. Owners are encouraged to coordinate the planning of the rear of buildings with adjacent neighbors.

Concerns

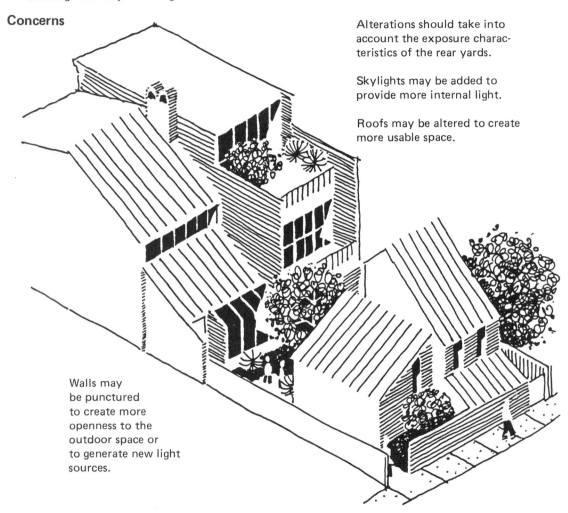

Alterations should take into account the exposure characteristics of the rear yards.

Skylights may be added to provide more internal light.

Roofs may be altered to create more usable space.

Walls may be punctured to create more openness to the outdoor space or to generate new light sources.

In cases where materials are removed from additions, they should be salvaged for use in new structures, in fences, or in outdoor landscape features.

Adjacent Units

Respect for the adjacent unit is mandatory. No alteration or addition will be permitted that intrudes on the light source of an adjacent unit. Owners are especially encouraged to coordinate the planning of additions with their neighbors.

Greenhouses

Inclusion of greenhouses in the rear is permitted. They may be attached to the structure or separate, they may be of wood or painted aluminum framing with glass (not plastic or polyurethane), and may be developed individually or from readily available kits. Care should be taken in terms of orientation, location and design in relation to the overall rear yard concept.

Terraces

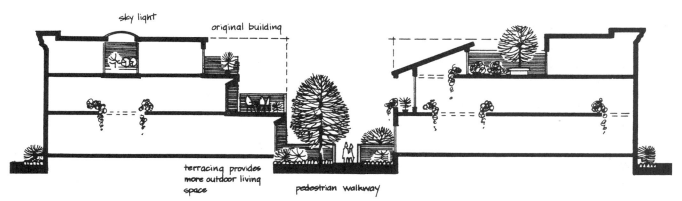

sky light

original building

terracing provides
more outdoor living
space

pedestrian walkway

Terrace

Transition

transition:
sculptural devices
to allow blending
of new architecture
with original

transition
area

original
unit

flush

corner

step

material

Attached Addition

Detached Addition

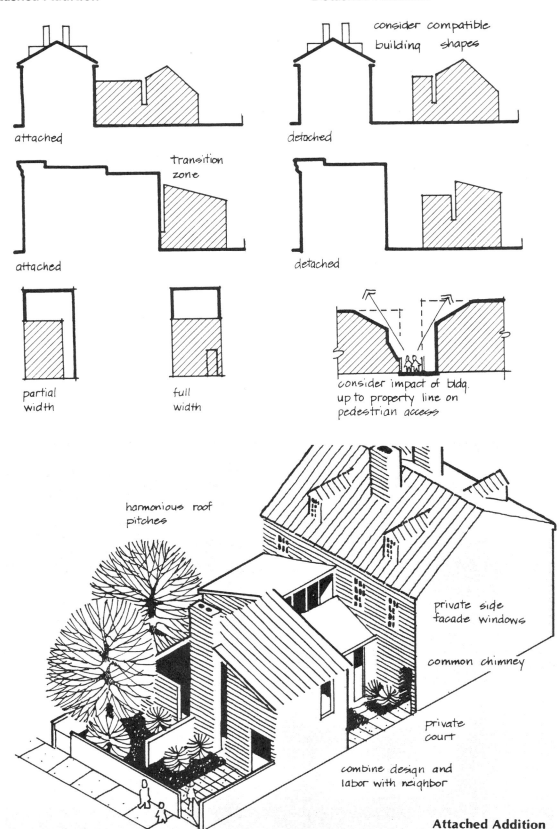

attached

detached

consider compatible
building shapes

transition zone

attached

detached

partial width

full width

consider impact of bldg.
up to property line on
pedestrian access

harmonious roof
pitches

private side
facade windows

common chimney

private court

combine design and
labor with neighbor

Attached Addition

Detached Addition

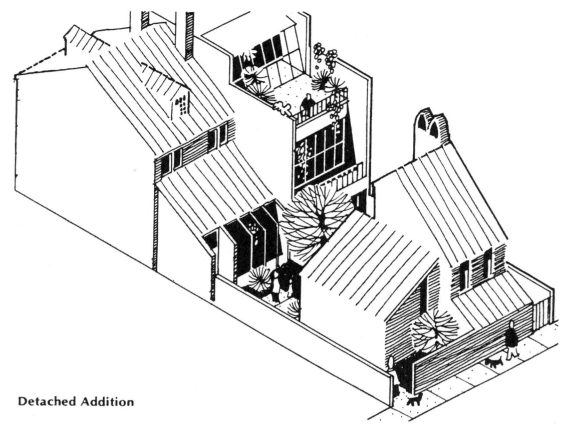

Detached Addition

Greenhouses

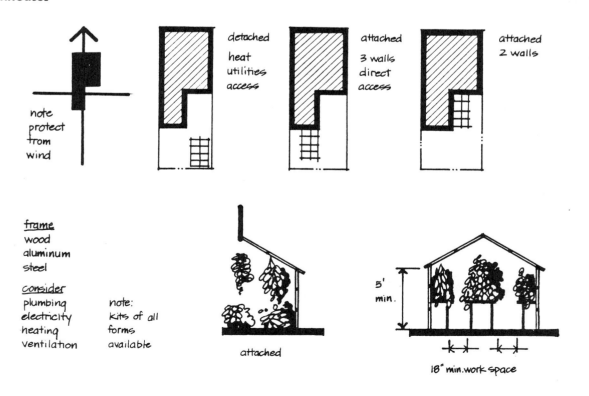

detached
heat
utilities
access

attached
3 walls
direct
access

attached
2 walls

note
protect
from
wind

<u>frame</u>
wood
aluminum
steel

<u>consider</u>
plumbing
electricity
heating
ventilation

note:
kits of all
forms
available

attached

5'
min.

18" min. work space

Roof area

Objective: To preserve original skyline and the design characteristics of roofs that are visible from the street.

STANDARDS:

1. Existing roof pitches, dormers and eaves on Federal Row units shall be retained and restored on front facades.

2. Existing fascias and cornices on Greek Revival units shall be restored or duplicated.

3. Existing chimneys visible on front facades shall be retained and restored to period style.

4. Roof materials on Federal Row units shall be standing-seam metal, dark shingles, slate, or fire-rated cedar shakes.

5. Gutters shall be of half-round design; downspouts and leaders shall be of round design; and all shall be copper or aluminum, or galvanized painted with dark colors.

The Federal Row pitched roofs and the Greek Revival cornices in an irregular pattern are the most frequent roof forms in the Otterbein area. The pitched roofs were distinguished by their simple materials with dormer windows and double chimney stacks, while the flat roof is distinguished by the more elaborate cornice detailing. Both the mass of the pitched roof and the cornice act as a termination of the building face. The design of such physical roof forms should be maintained and restored.

Cornices

The main cornice of the Otterbein Greek Revival units is generally constructed of wood, stone, brick or pressed metal. They were often elaborately ornamented and reflect in form and detailing specific architectural styles. Cornice lines emphasize the linear pattern of the streets and provide strong, visual termination of the building facades. Unless repair is completely unfeasible, originial cornices should not be removed from the buildings. On some units the cornices have been totally removed in more recent times. In those instances, an appropriately designed cornice should be added. If replacement or addition of the cornice is necessary, a suitably designed substitute should respect the correct proportions in massing, body and weight. The intricacy of detail is least important.

Pitched roofs

These roofs are an integral element of the Federal Row front facade and may require total rebuilding. Care should be taken that the original roof pitches are maintained. Acceptable roof materials are standing seam metal, dark shingles, slate or fire-rated cedar shakes.

Gutters and downspouts

Copper gutters and downspouts are suggested both for durability and appearance and should be allowed to weather naturally. If aluminum or galvanized steel are used, they should be painted in dark colors. Although installation on street facades of most Otterbein buildings is necessary, downspouts should be placed inconspicuously as, for example, along the line of the party wall.

Dormers

The dormer windows appear on the 2 and 3 story units only and are centered on the building face. Dormers should be maintained and repaired with suitable materials. The side should be of wood clapboard painted to match window color and the roof materials painted to match the main roof.

Chimneys

Chimneys are an integral part of the Federal Row houses and often appear as pairs on either side of the roof peak. They should be restored to the appropriate style and rebuilt with brick that matches the brick on the body of the unit.

In old houses the chimneys were constructed without flue linings or were lined with plaster. Lime mortar was not greatly affected by gases and condensation as long as wood was used as the fuel. However, as anthracite coal came to be used as a fuel, the mortar was seriously damaged.

Typical roof

Roofs take two forms in Barre Circle, the shed roof of Greek Revival units, which are not visible from the street and the visible pitched roofs of Federal period units. The roof, when visible acts as an upper terminus, framing the building face.

Structure

If roofs of Federal period units require rebuilding, attention should be given to preserve the original location and pitch. Greek Revival units, since they lack visible roofs, need to be concerned with preserving the skyline.

Materials

Original roof materials were cedar shakes for the majority of units and metal or slate for the more affluent. Cedar shakes are a fire hazard and unsuited for shallow pitches. Black tar and paper is incompatible because of their dirty appearance. Standing seam metal roofs and shingles provide a suitable texture and character.

Color

Roof materials which present a medium to dark background which complements the rest of the building are appropriate. The color should be darker than the sky and more neutral in hue so as not to compete with the front facade trim.

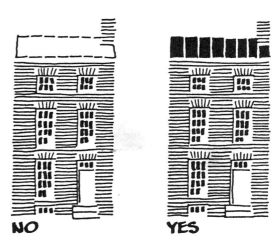

LIGHT and DARK ROOF MATERIALS

Eave design

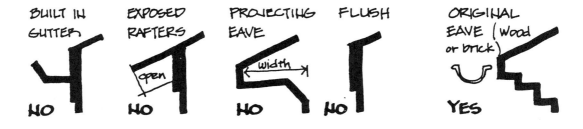

How to Make Cities Liveable

Otterbein - Cornice examples

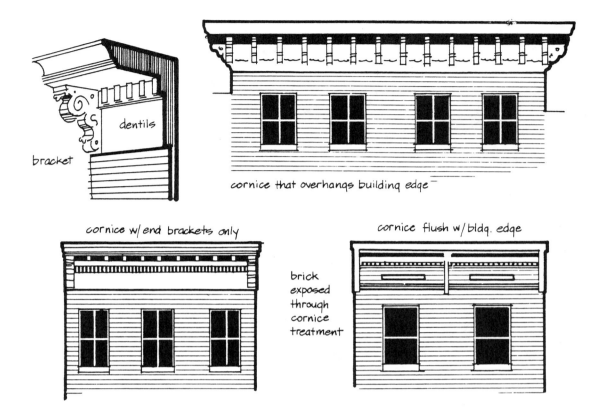

bracket

dentils

cornice that overhangs building edge

cornice w/ end brackets only

cornice flush w/ bldg. edge

brick exposed through cornice treatment

Cornice replacement

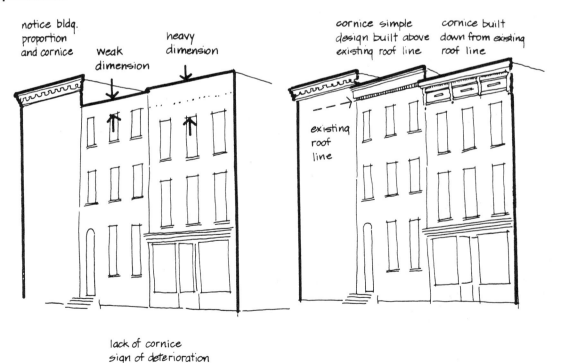

notice bldg. proportion and cornice

weak dimension

heavy dimension

cornice simple design built above existing roof line

cornice built down from existing roof line

existing roof line

lack of cornice sign of deterioration sterile facade

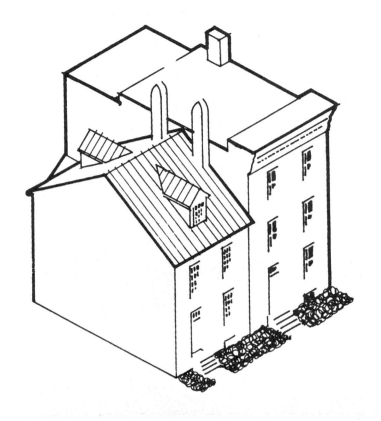

chimneys visible in front facade shall be restored

existing roof pitch dormers, eaves on federal period units to be restored

existing fascias and cornices on greek revival units shall be restored

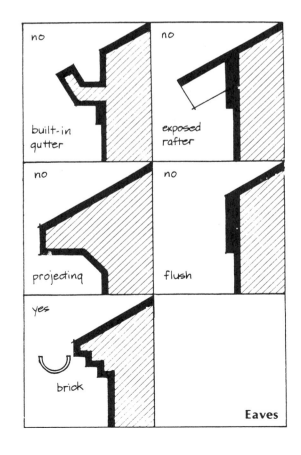

no — built-in gutter	no — exposed rafter
no — projecting	no — flush
yes — brick	

Eaves

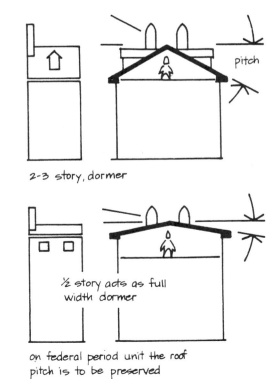

2-3 story, dormer

½ story acts as full width dormer

on federal period unit the roof pitch is to be preserved

pitch

Chimneys

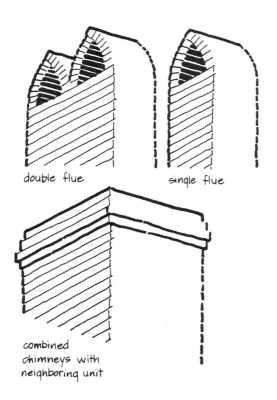

double flue

single flue

combined
chimneys with
neighboring unit

Dormers

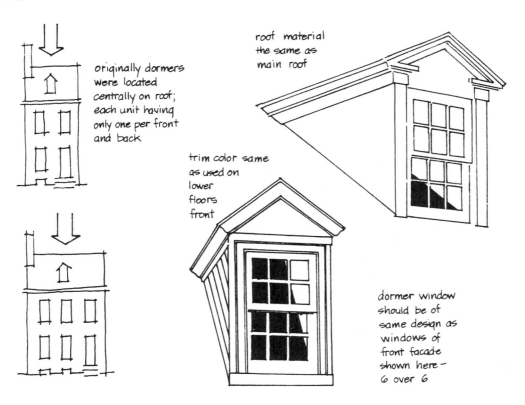

originally dormers
were located
centrally on roof;
each unit having
only one per front
and back

roof material
the same as
main roof

trim color same
as used on
lower
floors
front

dormer window
should be of
same design as
windows of
front facade
shown here -
6 over 6

Entrances

Objective: To preserve original design and positive elements of entrances and stoops.

STANDARDS:

1. Doors on front facades shall be wood panel construction in period style.

2. Existing transoms, and other embellishments characteristic of period style shall be retained, restored or duplicated.

3. Shutters shall be of louvered or paneled design, and painted wood construction and shall be one half the width of the opening and the same length as the opening.

4. Stoop materials shall be stone, wood or brick.

5. Cheek walls on stoops shall not be permitted.

6. Wrought iron railing shall be permitted for safety if dark in color, simple in design, and sturdy in appearance.

7. Exterior lighting of a design appropriate to the original architecture shall be above or flanking the front entrance.

The entrance to the Otterbein houses customarily included front stoops or entrance steps and the doorway, with accompanying wood paneling containing symmetrically designed ornamentation. The entrance areas were designed as a formal image to the street occurring at either street level or set above a low basement. They were sometimes simply designed or ornamented with flamboyant and individual embellishments.

If the entrance to an Otterbein residence is to remain as an impressive feature, as it was originally designed, it must be maintained and repaired with considerable care. Inappropriate alterations to any entrance will substantially affect the appearance of the building and can destroy the unity of an entire street facade.

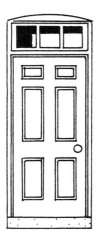

3 light transom to be restored
doors on front facade to be of wood panel construction in period design of building

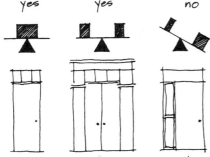

yes   yes   no

entrances should be restored to original symmetrical design

Doors

The original doors of the Otterbein residences were made of fine woods, handsomely paneled and occasionally adorned with ornate hardware. Replacement doors of paneled wood construction that maintain the proportions and form of the originals should be installed. Appropriate single door styles are 6 or 8 paneled doors in various designs without glazing.

The French door, a symmetrical double door opening at the center, is often appropriate in the Greek Revival units, and, if desired, may be fitted with symmetrically placed full length glass insets. Wherever possible, transoms and side lights should be retained intact.

Simple entrance

A simple entrance refers to one with a lack of embellishments found on both the Federal period units and the early Greek Revival units. The door casing contained a three-light transom above the opening, and the doors were 6 to 8 panels without glazing. Such entrances were simple functional statements.

In restoration of these entrances, the transom should follow the design of the windows on the rest of the front facade or three panes across. The color of the door casing should match that of the window casing.

Embellished entrance

This refers to those entrances which reflect classical architectural detailing and more elaborate ornamentation of the side columns and overhead lintels. These embellished entrances should be restored or duplicated, being very sensitive to the proportions and massing of forms, and particularly to the balanced relationship with the cornice detailing above.

Shutters and blinds

Originally, many Federal period units used shutters and blinds at the entrance areas. Shutters or blinds should only be used on those units with simple entrance detailing and should be of the same design, material and color as adjoining first floor window shutters. They should not open onto handrails, but return against the facade of the house. Non-functioning shutters must have appropriate hardware.

Hardware

Hardware refers to the functional and appointment elements of the entrance area such as doorknobs, house numbers, mail slots, mail boxes, entry lights and door knockers. If they are sensitively selected and placed, they can be an asset to the facade; if not, they can create an unnecessary clutter.

Hardware should be simple and clean in design. The most attractive materials are brass or bronze, but other metals painted a darker color can be appropriate.

House number should be in a type face that is simple and complements the unit. Written numbers are not appropriate.

Entry lights should be designed with clean, simple lines, large glass areas and vertical emphasis. Avoid large, riveted or hammered looks with eagle ornamentation.

Hardware location should be balanced with the entrance. The hardware should also balance with other hardware on adjoining units and avoid the appearance of clutter. Avoid placing hardware that appears like a spot, unrelated to anything else on a wall.

Stoops

The front stoops in the Otterbein area occur in a variety of forms at street level or set above a low basement with the entrance at mid-level. Traditional materials were wood and stone; brick may be considered acceptable, but usually is not desirable.

Many original steps were of wood and were removable in order to provide access to basement levels. Often they were open on the side to allow some light to the basement.

Patching or sealing of stone steps when required should be neatly executed and, if necessary, followed by a matte finish coat of paint. The painting should maintain the general color of the natural masonry and must not be completed in bright or unusual shades. Replacement steps of stone should be left in a natural state.

While brick is allowable, it is not encouraged in that it provides an inappropriate transition between the facade brick and the sidewalk paving.

Steps should be designed to be bracketed to the wall with a landing area provided at the entrance level. Risers must be closed at approximately 7 to 8 inches in height and may run perpendicular or parrallel to the front wall. Treads must be a minimum of 9 inches in width. Cheek walls are not acceptable.

Wrought iron handrails, where appropriate on multi-riser steps, should be of a clean simple design, sturdy in construction and appearance and dark in color. Avoid the use of ornate embellishments. Railings should be complementary and functional not flamboyant.

Area ways to basement levels may be retained or enclosed. Those that are retained should provide safety railings, lights and proper drainage, and should be enclosed with a simply designed wrought iron handrail around the opening. A simple gate may also be provided for safety.

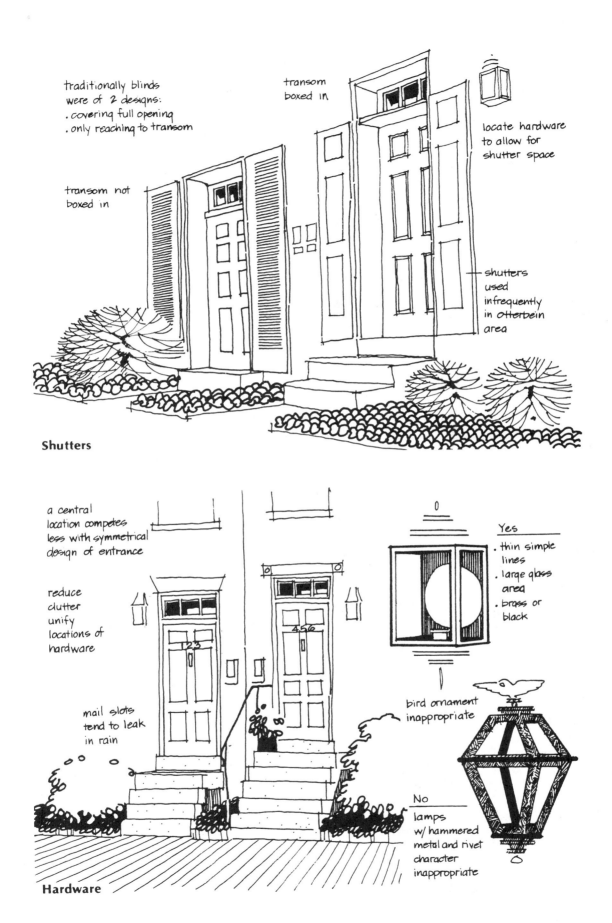

traditionally blinds
were of 2 designs:
. covering full opening
. only reaching to transom

transom not
boxed in

transom
boxed in

locate hardware
to allow for
shutter space

shutters
used
infrequently
in Otterbein
area

Shutters

a central
location competes
less with symmetrical
design of entrance

reduce
clutter
unify
locations of
hardware

mail slots
tend to leak
in rain

Yes
. thin simple
   lines
. large glass
   area
. brass or
   black

bird ornament
inappropriate

No
lamps
w/ hammered
metal and rivet
character
inappropriate

Hardware

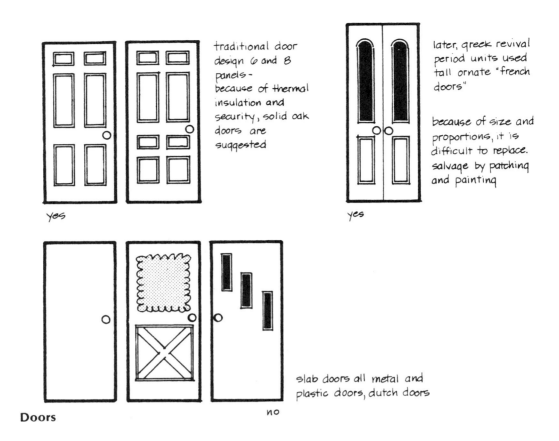

traditional door design 6 and 8 panels - because of thermal insulation and security, solid oak doors are suggested

yes

later, greek revival period units used tall ornate "french doors"

because of size and proportions, it is difficult to replace. salvage by patching and painting

yes

slab doors all metal and plastic doors, dutch doors

Doors

no

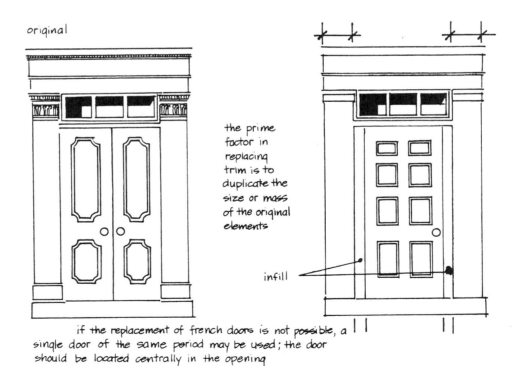

original

the prime factor in replacing trim is to duplicate the size or mass of the original elements

infill

if the replacement of french doors is not possible, a single door of the same period may be used; the door should be located centrally in the opening

Entrance Embellishments

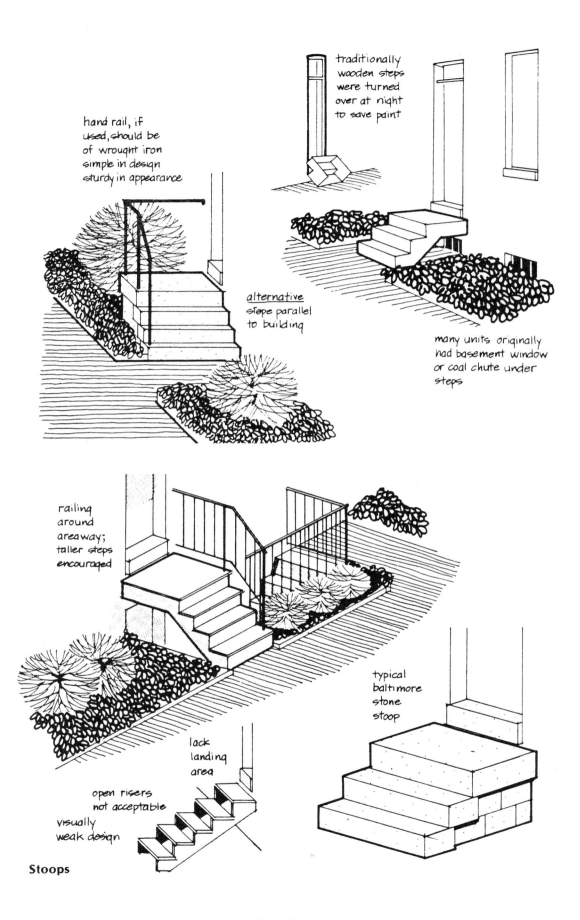

hand rail, if used, should be of wrought iron simple in design sturdy in appearance

alternative
steps parallel to building

traditionally wooden steps were turned over at night to save paint

many units originally had basement window or coal chute under steps

railing around areaway; taller steps encouraged

lack landing area

open risers not acceptable

visually weak design

typical baltimore stone stoop

Stoops

The entrance area in Barre Circle rowhouses includes the openings, the door, stoop and hardware. Traditionally the entrance areas were designed to have a formal appearance. They were clean, symmetrical arrangements with few embellishments and should be continued as such.

Focal point

The entrance acts as a focal point. It is a small element of the block facade and takes on more importance as you approach the unit, and its visual impact upon entering the building is very significant. Small items have great impact when they are located in the entrance area.

Design

A majority of the entrances in Barre Circle were simple single door designs. The casing contained a three-light transom above the opening, doors were solid wood, 6 or 8 panel construction without glazing and painted the same color as the windows.

Ornament

In restoration of these entrances the transom should follow the design of the windows on the rest of the front facade. Six over six windows would have a three-light transom.

For the few embellished entrances which reflect classical architectural detailing, they should be restored or replaced, being very sensitive to the proportions, massing, and balanced relationship of ornamentation.

TYPICAL ENTRANCES WITH THREE LIGHT TRANSOM AND 6-8 PANELED DOORS.

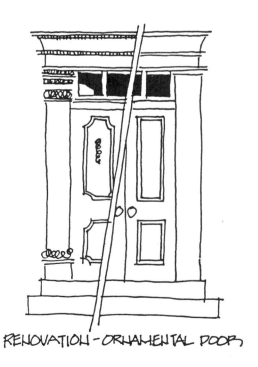

RENOVATION - ORNAMENTAL DOOR

Doors

YES   YES   YES

APPROPRIATE DOOR DESIGNS FOR
FEDERAL and EARLY GREEK REVIVAL UNITS
TYPICAL 6 and 8 PANELED DOORS.

YES   YES

FRENCH DOORS - LATER
GREEK REVIVAL

NO   NO   NO

INAPPROPRIATE DOOR DESIGNS

infill

dutch
door
vents

NO   NO

The original doors of Barre Circle rowhouses were made of solid wood, handsomely paneled and occasionally adorned with ornate hardware. Replacement doors of paneled wood construction that maintains the proportions and form of the originals should be installed, as shown above. Glazing is appropriate only in the French doors of Greek Revival units.

Symmetry

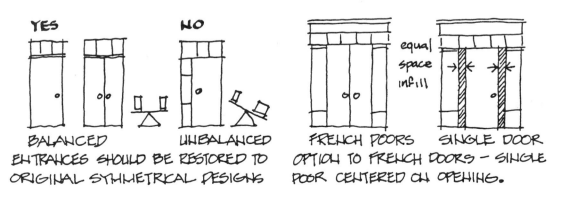

YES   NO

BALANCED   UNBALANCED
ENTRANCES SHOULD BE RESTORED TO
ORIGINAL SYMMETRICAL DESIGNS

equal
space
infill

FRENCH DOORS   SINGLE DOOR
OPTION TO FRENCH DOORS - SINGLE
DOOR CENTERED ON OPENING.

Stoop

A majority of units have shallow basements and require steps to enter the first floor. These steps - or stoop areas - have a special heritage in Baltimore. Their maintenance, especially those made of marble was, and is presently a sign of neighborhood pride. Stoops can also function as a social gathering place, a piece of playground equipment, or a quiet place to relax and watch the city.

Design

Because of the scale and simplicity of the architecture, a clean, functional series of risers look best. Be sure to check with city code requirements.

If existing stone steps are damaged, patch and paint with matte finish stone color.

TYPICAL BALTIMORE MARBLE STOOP

stoop centered on entrance

reveal

Open landing

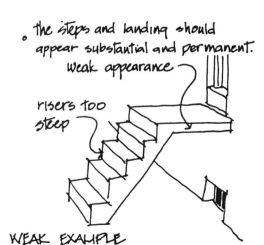

the steps and landing should appear substantial and permanent.

weak appearance

risers too steep

WEAK EXAMPLE

some existing steps may cover basement windows

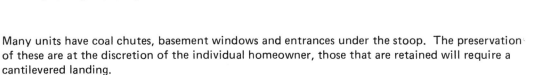

Many units have coal chutes, basement windows and entrances under the stoop. The preservation of these are at the discretion of the individual homeowner, those that are retained will require a cantilevered landing.

Stoops - Typical example

Handrails should only be used when required by code. A block with handrails on each unit can appear busy.

Handrails should be simple in design, made of wrought iron and painted a gloss black.

Treads and risers appear best with a reveal along the side - to look as if they are floating over the base.

Wrought iron steps are esthetically inappropriate for Barre Circle rowhouses. The busy airy feeling of iron step designs look out of place.

SIMPLE DESIGNS USING APPROPRIATE MATERIALS MAKE BEST SOLUTIONS

Areaways

PRESERVATION OF AREAWAYS IS OPTION OF RESIDENT

Codes will require a handrail for steps above a specific height and in areaway situations.

Adequate lighting and drainage should be provided in under-step areaways.

Stoops above areaways should have a substantial appearance to give a feeling of strength.

Curbs should be provided to stop water and trash from collecting at the bottom of areaways.

Stoop materials

The traditional stoop materials were stone and wood. Wood is considered inappropriate because of its temporary appearance. It is recommended that materials more substantial in appearance and lighter in color be used, for example, stone and concrete should be used for the treads, this accentuates the entrance area against the darker color of the brick walls. Precast concrete steps are inappropriate because of scale and detailing. They were designed for suburban homes.

Brick treads

Brick treads give a feeling of the entrance door floating in the brick wall and are not recommended. The light color of the stone adds emphasis to the entrance.

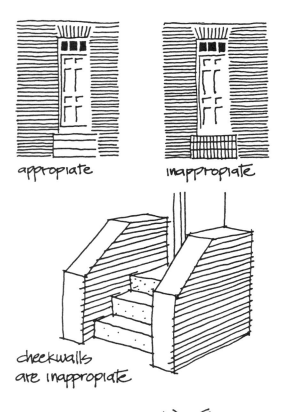

appropiate   inappropiate

cheekwalls
are inappropiate

Cheekwalls

Cheekwalls for stoops appear too large and heavy. They are out of place in front of row housing.

Orientation

Originally the entrances were perpendicular to the building, and this practice should be continued where possible. But for the few units requiring many risers to enter an acceptable alternative would be to turn the steps so that they ran parallel to the building. This would prevent the stoop from projecting too far into the sidewalk area.

Hardware

Entrance hardware refers to items such as doorknobs, house numbers, mail slots, mail boxes, entry lights, door knockers, etc. If they are sensitively selected and placed, they can be an asset to the front facade; if not, they can create an unnecessary clutter.

The small elements of the entrance have a great visual impact on the viewer.

House numbers

House numbers should be in a type face that is simple and legible. Written numbers are inappropriate.

Numbers should be centered on the entrance opening.

Hardware should be simple and clean in design. The most attractive materials are brass or bronze, but painted metal can be appropriate if dark colors are used.

Design

Hardware location should be balanced with the entrance to avoid the appearance of clutter. Centering objects gives the feeling of stability. For example, locate the house light half way between the window and the door at transom level. All house lights should be attached to the architecture.

Location

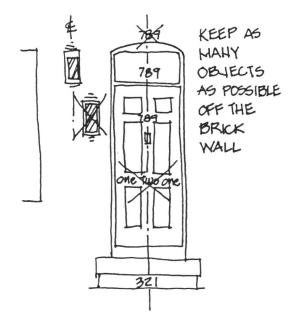

KEEP AS MANY OBJECTS AS POSSIBLE OFF THE BRICK WALL

Shutters

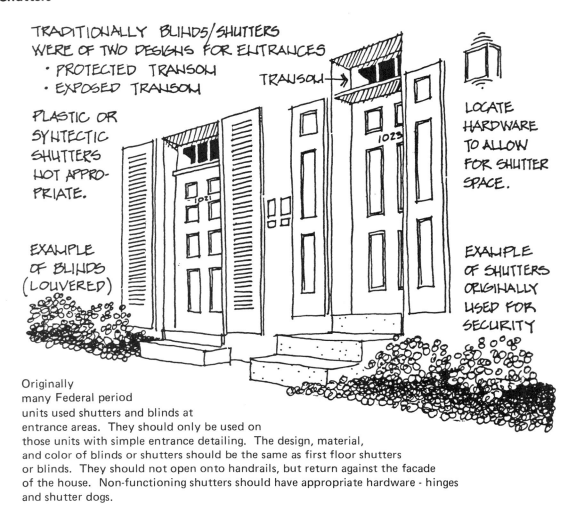

TRADITIONALLY BLINDS/SHUTTERS WERE OF TWO DESIGNS FOR ENTRANCES
- PROTECTED TRANSOM
- EXPOSED TRANSOM

PLASTIC OR SYNTECTIC SHUTTERS NOT APPROPRIATE.

EXAMPLE OF BLINDS (LOUVERED)

TRANSOM →

LOCATE HARDWARE TO ALLOW FOR SHUTTER SPACE.

EXAMPLE OF SHUTTERS ORIGINALLY USED FOR SECURITY

Originally
many Federal period
units used shutters and blinds at
entrance areas. They should only be used on
those units with simple entrance detailing. The design, material,
and color of blinds or shutters should be the same as first floor shutters
or blinds. They should not open onto handrails, but return against the facade
of the house. Non-functioning shutters should have appropriate hardware - hinges
and shutter dogs.

Design

All shutter or blinds should be of one design
and color.

SHUTTER WIDTH EQUAL ½ WIDTH DOOR OPENING. SHUTTERS (BLINDS) SHOULD FULLY OPEN.

The installation of handrails eliminates the
option of installing shutters.

Walls/brick

Objective: To restore and to preserve original brick surfaces.

STANDARDS:

1. Existing brick surfaces on front facades shall be restored and preserved.

2. All surface coverings on front, including but not limited to "formstone" or stucco, shall be removed and underlying brick surfaces shall be repaired and preserved.

3. Side and rear facades shall be restored to original brick surfaces whenever possible.

4. Deteriorated or missing brickwork shall be repaired to be inconspicuous and compatible with existing brickwork in size, texture, bond and color.

5. The preservation of raw brick surfaces shall be attained without the use of paint.

The elements of architecture set against raw brick walls most exemplify the character of Otterbein and are one of the prime considerations of restoration.

The quality of brick varies throughout Otterbein with many of the fronts of a high quality and harder brick, and some fronts and most sides and rears having a lesser quality and more porous brick. Some of the original brick has been covered with stucco.

Cleaning

Cleaning should be undertaken if the appearance of a building is substantially affected by dirt or staining. In many instances, brick masonry can be steam cleaned. However, encrusted dirt may necessitate the use of water under controlled pressure or water and fine sand used in combination. Cleaning by sandblasting is generally not recommended in that it is abrasive and may remove mortar or damage the brick surface. Sandblasting may be required to remove paint from masonry surfaces, but should not be used until it is determined that no damage to the brick surface will result. Stains like those under copper downspouts or fire escapes may require chemical treatment. The process should be supervised by an experienced contractor.

After cleaning, the brick surfaces may be protected against the effects of weathering and dirt accumulation by waterproofing with silicone.

Repairing

While repairing a section of deteriorated wall, attention should be given to matching adjoining bricks with bricks of the same size, texture and color, and utilizing the same technique and bonding method. The bonding method generally found in the Otterbein area is Flemish or common.

Mortar

In order to achieve a richly textured brick wall, it is often better to use a grey or darker tinted mortar when repointing so that the wall itself is emphasized rather then the individual bricks. When a light tone mortar is used, each brick seems to stand out separately. The use of darker mortar is also appropriate when introducing areas or panels of new brick work in a remodeling job. The darker mortar helps the new work relate better to the old by producing a similar richness of effect, even if the color of the bricks may be quite different.

Much of the existing mortar in Otterbein is of lime and sand, and is soft; the color is the result of the specific sand used. An analysis of the existing mortar to determine the ingredients aids in matching the color.

It is best to repoint the mortar having the same density and absorbency as the bricks themselves. Soft brick and stone should be repointed with soft mortar, as hard mortar will cause the softer brick to disintegrate.

Repointing

Much of the brick masonry in Otterbein was laid up with a variety of joints varying from 1/8'' to 3/8'' of thickness. In repointing the brick, one should strive for an inconspicuous appearance. Mortar can easily be colored to match that of the original construction. Joints should be raked, tooled, scored or otherwise treated in order to match original joint techniques.

Preservatives

Deterioration of brick surfaces can be abated through the application of silicones and other recently developed waterproofing preservatives. Silicones are invisible and produce a chemical bond that protects the wall from moisture and sun. The application of silicones requires the advice and supervision of a waterproofing expert, and should be undertaken after a building has been cleaned or repaired. The preservative effect of silicones will last for several years.

Repair

When repairing sections of brick wall, there are several things to watch out for:

1. New bricks should be selected to match the originals in size, shape, texture and color.

2. New mortar should match the existing mortar in both color and texture. If the entire wall is to be repointed, color and texture are the owners option.

3. When repointing a section of wall, mortar joints should be shaped to match the existing. When repointing an entire wall, mortar shape is the owners option.

4. Repairing a wall section will also require continuing the existing bonding method.

Mortar

An analysis of the existing mortar to determine the ingredients aids in matching color. It is best to repoint with mortar having the same density and absorbancy as the bricks themselves. Soft brick and stone should be repointed with soft mortar, as hard mortar will cause the softer brick to disintegrate.

Preservatives

Deterioration of brick surfaces can be abated through the application of silicones or other recently developed waterproof preservatives. Application should be undertaken after the building has been cleaned and repaired. The preservative effect of silicones will last for several years.

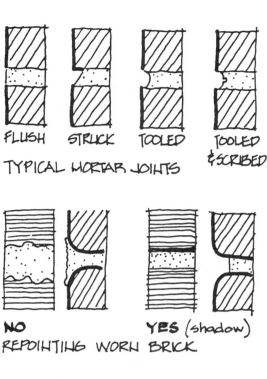

FLUSH STRUCK TOOLED TOOLED & SCRIBED

TYPICAL MORTAR JOINTS

NO   YES (shadow)

REPOINTING WORN BRICK

STIPPLING TO ACHIEVE TEXTURE

TRADITIONAL white mortar   CONTEMPORARY Tinted mortar

MORTAR COLOR — OPTION

FLEMISH BOND   COMMON BOND

WHITE MORTAR APPEARS BUSY   TINTED MORTAR WALL READS.

Period architectural appointments set against uninterrupted brick walls most exemplify the character of Barre Circle. Brick is both esthetically and structurally of a prime concern in renovation of the architecture. Despite the initial cost of restoring brick walls, its maintenance and life expectancy will prove very economical.

Design

The original flat planar quality of walls should be retained. The use of bay windows, porches, wrought iron catwalks and other such appurtanences are all extremely inappropriate means to express individual tastes or to provide relief to continuous block walls.

Cleaning

Cleaning should be undertaken if the appearance of the building is substantially stained, dirty or painted. In many instances, brick masonry can be steam cleaned. Encrusted dirt may require the use of fine sand and water under controlled pressure. Cleaning by sand blasting is generally not recommended. It is abrasive and may remove mortar and damage the hardened crust on the existing bricks. Sandblasting can remove paint from masonry surfaces, but first it must be determined that no damage will result to the brick.

Stains

Stains, like those under down spouts may require chemical treatment. This process should be supervised.

Preservatives

After cleaning, the brick surfaces may be protected against the effects of dirt and weathering with clean silicone preservatives.

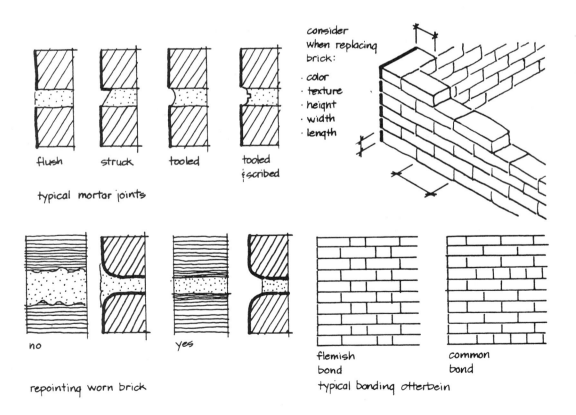

flush   struck   tooled   tooled & scribed

typical mortar joints

consider when replacing brick:
· color
· texture
· height
· width
· length

no   yes

repointing worn brick

flemish bond   common bond

typical bonding otterbein

Windows

Otterbein windows are usually vertically proportioned openings emphasized by lintels and sills with a minimum of embellishments. Windows vary in form with the architectural style of the building, and change in height and proportion with the functional importance of the rooms within. In Otterbein, windows were almost always double hung and the window configurations that were historically correct were 6 over 6 style for Federal Row houses and 6 over 6 style for the early Greek Revival units. The 2 over 2 and 1 over 1 styles were found in the later Greek Revival units and Federal Row modifications.

Objective: To preserve original window openings, casings and sash on front facade and, as often as practical, on side and rear facades.

STANDARDS:

1. Window style on front facade of Federal Row(pitched roof) shall be 6 over 6 or 1 over 1 with horizontal and vertical muntin arrangement.

2. Window style on front facade of Greek Revival(flat root) shall be 6 over 6, 2 over 2, or 1 over 1 with horizontal and vertical muntin arrangement.

3. Dormer windows on front facade shall match style of lower floors.

4. All window casings, sash, and muntins shall be painted or vinyl-clad wood.

5. Exterior storm windows on front facades shall not be permitted.

6. Exterior storm windows on other facades shall be painted or vinyl-clad wood, or painted or anodized aluminum.

7. Infilling of window openings to accommodate standard or stock window units shall not be permitted on front facades.

8. Infilling of window openings shall not be permitted on other facades if the standard window approximate the window opening size and proportion.

9. Shutters shall be of louvered or paneled design, and painted wood construction and shall be one half the width of the opening and the same length as the opening.

10. Shutters on front facades shall be installed on all floors or first floor only.

11. Wrought iron "burglar bars" shall be allowed.

12. Snap in mullions on front facades are not acceptable.

Inventory of sills and lintels

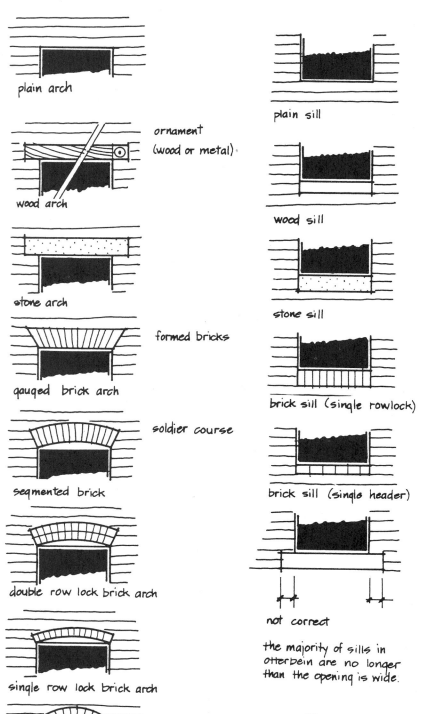

plain arch

ornament (wood or metal)

wood arch

stone arch

formed bricks

gauged brick arch

soldier course

segmented brick

double row lock brick arch

single row lock brick arch

roman or semi-circular brick arch

plain sill

wood sill

stone sill

brick sill (single rowlock)

brick sill (single header)

not correct

the majority of sills in otterbein are no longer than the opening is wide.

When modifying original sills and lintels, a survey of similar units of the same period should be taken to determine a suitable design. All sills on the front facade and side facades located on street corners should be of one design.

Shutters and blinds

Shutters refer to the paneled units originally employed for security reasons. Blinds refer to the louvered units originally used for shade, ventilation and security. In most cases, the latter units or blinds were not originally used in Otterbein.

Shutters or blinds shall be made of wood and are to be the full length of the opening and one half the width. If the installed shutters or blinds are not made workable, they must at least have the appropriate hardware such as hinges, catches and shutter dogs.

Alterations

Windows on the side facades facing vehicular and pedestrian alleyways may utilize standard available windows in the original openings by the use of infilling. Such windows should respect the style and proportion of those windows on the front facades. Burglar bars are acceptable and should be simple of design, sturdy in appearance and painted black. Wire mesh is not permitted.

Burglar bars

Wrought iron burglar bars are acceptable and should be of a simple design and gloss black in color. Wire mesh or industrial screening is not an appropriate window covering.

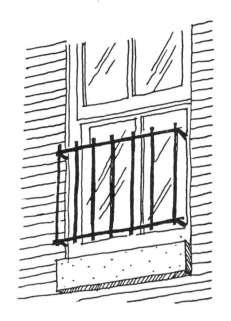

Window combinations

Lowered ceilings

When ceiling levels are to be lowered, consider the complications of ceilings that are placed lower than the window head height. If this is unavoidable, many alternatives which block the ceiling on the interior are possible, filling the window opening is unacceptable.

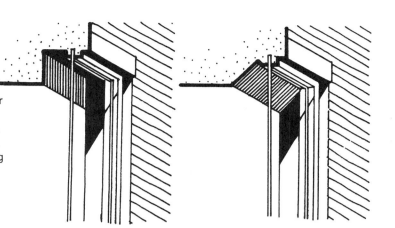

Window style

Windows should be double hung, of thin lined design with thin mullions. Snap-in mullions are not allowed on the front facade. Storm windows are not allowed on the front facades. An alternative to storm windows on the front facade is for the provision of storm windows on the inside, double glazing, or thermal curtains. Of those storm windows that are allowed on side and rear facades, a thin line style should be chosen in order to reduce their impact. If aluminum is chosen as material for the window, it should be painted the same color as the window casing.

Windows in the dormers and basements on the front facades should be of the same design, material and color as the major windows on the facade.

blinds   blinds   shutters

traditional blinds and shutters of federal period and later

Lintels and sills

In Otterbein the lintels and sills come in a variety of sizes, shapes and materials. The Federal Row units have simpler brick span lintels; the Greek Revival used other materials that are more prominent and are often embellished. Lintels and sills should be restored and repaired to the original style wherever possible. In those instances where lintels or sills do not exist, or they are beyond repair, it is permissible to duplicate a lintel or sill from a similar period building. Lintels should be reinforced with steel angles.

Openings

Window openings should not be enlarged, closed off or otherwise altered in form on front facades. New sashes for these windows should be cut to fit curved or irregular openings and should not be reduced for stock sizes or shapes. However, on side and rear facades, the openings may be altered or infilled to accommodate standard window casings.

Historically, the window sashes were painted in light colors such as white beige, light grey or cream. Wooden window frames should be the same color as the moveable sash.

arch or lintel

mullion

sash

pane of glazing

casing

sill

Window Panes

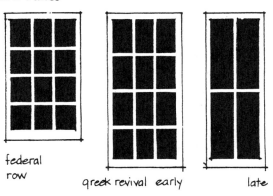

federal row

greek revival early

late

acceptable

all windows should be double hung painted wood or perma shield or equal

snap in mullions unacceptable

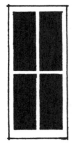

yes

no

thin line mullion correct for both federal row and greek revival unit

Shutters

BLINDS BLINDS SHUTTERS

Arrangement

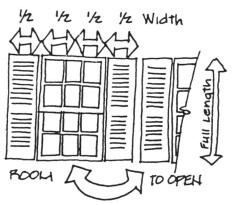

½ ½ ½ ½ Width

Full Length

ROOM TO OPEN

SHUTTERS AND BLINDS SHOULD BE
½ THE WIDTH AND FULL LENGTH
OF THE WINDOW OPENING

Traditional blinds and shutter designs

Although thought of today as decorative elements, shutters(paneled) and blinds(louvered), if functional, can provide shade, ventilation and security, as originally intended. They shall be made of painted wood and be the correct size and shape for the window openings. If installed, they should appear functional with appropriate hardware -hinges, catches and dogs.

Design and material

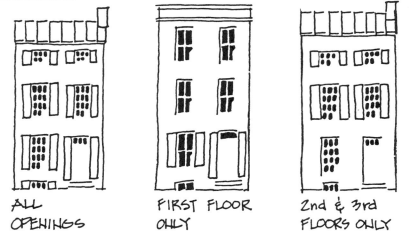

ALL OPENINGS   FIRST FLOOR ONLY   2nd & 3rd FLOORS ONLY   WINDOWS ONLY

Typical combinations of shutters and blinds

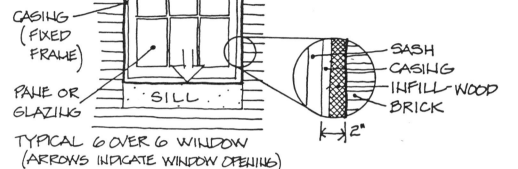

LINTEL (ARCH DESIGN SHOWN)

MULLION

SASH (THE SLIDING FRAME)

CASING (FIXED FRAME)

PANE OR GLAZING

SILL

TYPICAL 6 OVER 6 WINDOW
(ARROWS INDICATE WINDOW OPENING)

SASH
CASING
INFILL-WOOD
BRICK

|← →| 2"

Double hung

All front facade and street corner facade windows shall be double hung design, except in instances where a single pane fixed glass is used.

Material

All front facade and street corner side facade window casings, sashes, and mullions shall be painted or vinyl clad wood.

Standard windows

In instances where standard windows are planned for the front facade and street corner side facades the casing infill shall not exceed (2) inches on any side of a window opening.

Lintels and sills

When lintels or sills are beyond repair or nonexistent it is permissible to copy designs from similar period buildings in the Barre Circle area.

Opening relocation

In instances where the window openings are inconsistent from the original design intent, the owner has the option to preserve or correct the inconsistency, after first receiving permission from the architectural review committee.

WINDOW OPENING INCONSISTENCIES MAY BE CORRECTED.

Acceptable designs

Acceptable window styles shall be double hung - 6 over 6, 2 over 2, 1 over 1, and single fixed panes.

Historically correct window styles would be 2 over 2 for the tall proportioned windows of later Greek Revival units, and 6 over 6 windows for the shorter openings of Federal period and early Greek Revival units.

The 1 over 1 fixed single pane style window offers practical solutions. The single pane design gives an attractive contemporary flavor which would complement the architecture.

The residents who have a Federal style window, but the openings are taller, then a 9 over 6 may be appropriate, approval of this design exception must come from the architectural review board.

Unacceptable designs

4 over 4 window designs are not acceptable because the proportions of individual panes are horizontal in emphasis.

9 over 9, 12 over 12 and other multi-pane style windows are unacceptable because they represent and earlier colonial period.

Historically correct designs

The only historically correct architectural styles which are appropriate for Barre Circle rowhouses are either Federal Period or Greek Revival designs. Renovation or restoration of each of the units should conform to the original design guidelines for components on units of those types.

6 OVER 6
FEDERAL PERIOD

6 OVER 6
Early GREEK REVIVAL

2 OVER 2
Late GREEK REVIVAL

9 OVER 6

1 OVER 1

FIXED GLASS

POOR DESIGN
NO - HORIZONTAL PROPORTIONS

COLONIAL
WRONG PERIOD
NO

FEDERAL PERIOD

GREEK REVIVAL

Color

The use of color in architecture is always an emotional, controversial subject. Personal taste, current fashion, out-doing the neighbors and a fear of reprisal are just a few of the criteria which dictate color selection, justified or unjustified. The Barre Circle residents have, by electing to restore brick surfaces, determined the predominant unifying color of the neighborhood and the more traditional character of the architecture. The following are a few general principles concerning the use of color in renovation and restoration in the Barre Circle area:

Graphics

With a traditional use of color, the architectural designs and details will relate to the original function. Doors will look like doors, windows will look like windows and buildings will appear as architecture, not a painting or graphic.

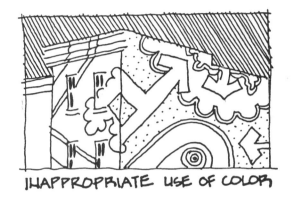

INAPPROPRIATE USE OF COLOR

Environment

REGIONAL INFLUENCE OF COLOR

Color should relate to the environment, landscape and climate of the area. In the past this was accomplished when indigenous materials - brick, stone, wood, were used. Consequently materials and colors which are alien to the environment should be avoided, e.g. aluminum, plastic, chrome, imitation materials.

Local color

Natural, muted colors, earth tones, such as warm grey, blue grey, beige, terra cotta, olive, cream, and tan are examples of colors that relate well to the local environs, climate and seasonal changes. Pastels, powdery, pale color - pink, pale yellows, lavender are all more appropriate in sunny climates which last year round, and are less appropriate for temperate climates, over-cast weather, and the seasonal changes in color.

Typical areas of color

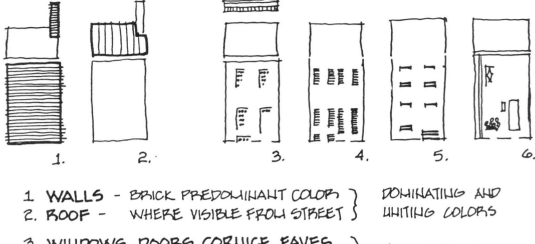

1. **WALLS** - BRICK PREDOMINANT COLOR ⎤
2. **ROOF** - WHERE VISIBLE FROM STREET ⎦ DOMINATING AND UNITING COLORS

3. **WINDOWS, DOORS, CORNICE, EAVES** ⎤
4. **SHUTTERS** - OPTIONAL ⎟
5. **SILLS, LINTELS, STOOP, OTHER** ⎟ ELEMENTS THAT EMPHASIZE, HARMONIZE AND COMPLIMENT.
6. **MISCELLANEOUS** - DOWNSPOUT FLOWER BOX, WINDOW CURTAIN, DOOR. OTHER ⎦

The above illustrates a typical unit divided into potential areas of individual color. The following section will discuss each of the above areas in greater detail.

Walls

Walls- Architectural standards, developed by the Barre Circle residents, requires that brick surfaces be retained and restored. Brick will therefore be the predominant and unifying color of the neighborhood. The brick colors generally range from dark red to salmon.

Repair

In repairing portions of a wall care shold be taken to match existing brick and mortar. If repairing a whole wall consider using a grey or earth color tinted mortar which is closer in color to brick, but never darker. The traditional use of lighter color mortar tends to emphasize each brick, especially where joints of 1/4" to 1/2" were used, giving a busy appearance. Darker mortar creates a more unified surface.

Shutters/blinds

Since shutters and blinds would comprise a large area of the building facade, white, black and earth tones offer an appropriate color selection. Bright hues of red, orange, blue, and pastels tend to appear commercial. Traditional colors were dark greens and black.

All shutters and blinds on one building should be of one color.

Sills, lintels and stoops

Sills, lintels, and stoops should reflect original treatment. Stone should be repaired and if necessary painted to match original raw color. Brick should be repaired to retain raw brick texture and match wall color.

Hardware

Elements such as utility equipment, vents, meters should be a flat color which blends with wall surface. Burglar bars, hand rails and other iron work should be painted black gloss finish.

Contiguous unit

original wood lintels painted light grey to imitate stone

hand rail, burglar bars, simple design, gloss black

It is recommended that color be divided into two areas of concern:

individual color choice for doors, shutters, blinds, hardware, stoops,

group choice for cornice, eaves, windows, and window and door casings.

Windows, doors and trim

Windows, doors, cornices, eaves, etc. tend to emphasize, harmonize, or complement the predominant brick color. Light colors contrast and sparkle, while the earth colors blend and offer a more unified appearance - of wall and trim. Dark colors are heavier and more reserved in appearance. All are appropriate.

All the windows, window and door casings and cornice should be one color.

Do not use bright hues of orange, yellow, red, blue, green, etc.

Windows - Light and dark

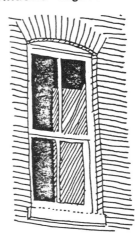

Dark colors give appearance of bars on windows

lighter colors give sparkle to window, and from interior mullions are less apparent.

Lighter colors contrast with darker areas of glass. They appear lively and cheerful even on overcast days.

Darker colors remove liveliness or overall character, give a more reserved appearance.

Entrances

Entrances can visually act as a focal point and have a variety of color options, keep in mind the impact to neighborhood image. The door frame should match window colors while the door itself may be treated individually.

Cornices - modeling and detail can be emphasized by light colors, sun and shadow. Dark colors tend to mute and render invisible the fine details.

Dark cornice heavy & details are hidden

door act as a focal point

Painting walls

When the existing raw brick is an unattractive color or the wall has been repaired in the past with an unmatched brick, painting the wall may be an alternative to replacing the brick. Painted brick work generally requires repainting every five years.

the exception may prove the rule

Individual unit

For units that are individual in design, compared to adjoining units earthy colors other than red might be considered.

Contiguous unit

For units that are part of a contiguous group colors should match or blend with adjacent units.

Roofs

NO
ROOF APPEAR
WEAK LIGHT

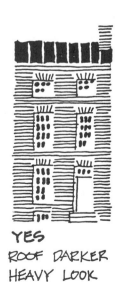

YES
ROOF DARKER
HEAVY LOOK

The following is referring to units which have roofs visible from the street.

The standards recommend a medium to dark (not black) roofing material.

Colors relating to original materials look appropriate: slate blue, greys, browns.

Environmentally a medium color will absorb heat in winter but not be uncomfortable in summer.

Bright colors

Colors of bright or intense hues, should be used in limited amounts as in nature as a device to focus attention, or to complement larger areas of natural colors.

Number of colors

The number of colors used per unit should be kept to a minimum, as the number increases coordination is complicated and the results appear busy.

Examples

Try to find examples of your color preference in use on similar architecture before making final selection.

Darker colors tend to recede and lighter colors come forward and enlarge appearance.

Finish

High gloss paint shows up imperfections in surfaces through reflections - matte finish may collect dirt, grime and pollutants and be difficult to maintain. Semi-gloss finish is recommended especially for high maintenance surfaces such as doors.

Dirt

Consider colors which show little dirt and thus require less maintenance.

Shadows

Notice orientation of building to determine shaded walls - especially north walls. Color appears less intense in shadows. This is important for units with fronts facing north.

UNITS FACING NORTH REMEMBER FACADE AWAYS IN SHADOW

Color chart

Suggested trim and detail color range	Relationship to brick surface
Cool white	Cold appliance-like look, beware of large areas of this color.
Warm white	
Cream	When in doubt - these are safe contrasts with brick color.
Light grey	
Beige	
Earth tones of;	Closer to tone of brick, and brick trim - less definition - both read as one - unity.
Reds	
Greens	
Blues	
Browns	
Williamsburg colors	
Dark tone of;	
Reds	Contrast with brick but less defined as light color - trim appears light.
Greens	
Blues	
Browns	
Greys	
Black	Detail relief, e.g., cornices lose definition - metalic appearance. Gloss black for metal hardware recommended.

Contemporary Conveniences

One aspect of architecture which many times receives inadequate consideration and yet has significant impact to appearance, is the design and placement of hardware, for example - air conditioning, utility lines, downspouts, etc. The objective with Barre Circle traditional architecture is to de-emphasize all the contemporary facilities which for practical reasons must be exposed.

Vent stacks, downspouts, chimneys, and other exterior hardware, if haphazardly located detract from the architectural appearance.

AWNINGS SHOULD BE CANVAS AND SIMPLE IN DESIGN.

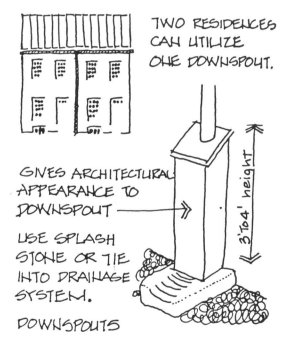

TWO RESIDENCES CAN UTILIZE ONE DOWNSPOUT.

GIVES ARCHITECTURAL APPEARANCE TO DOWNSPOUT →

USE SPLASH STONE OR TIE INTO DRAINAGE SYSTEM.

DOWNSPOUTS

3'to4' height

Awnings offer practical protection from the sun, especially for those units which face the evening or late afternoon sun. Canvas units of simple design and complementary color are recommended. They are easy to collapse and remove, during the cooler seasons. Metal units and prefabricated designs are out of character with the Barre Circle traditional theme.

It is recommended that downspouts and gutters be combined with those of adjoining units, where possible, to reduce the busy appearance on the block facade. They should be painted a medium to dark color to blend with their surroundings. Light, bright trim colors give too great an emphasis to the gutters and downspouts which appear against the darker brick color.

Downspouts should be combined and occur at building joint lines.

Objective: **To minimize the impact of contemporary services on original building design.**

STANDARDS:

1. Window air conditioning units or condenser elements shall not be permitted on front facades.

2. Television or radio antennas shall not be permitted where visible on front facades.

Installation of utility equipment on the exterior of any building in the Otterbein area should be restricted to the rear of the building or portions of the roof that are not visible from the street. Whenever possible, duplication of individual utility units should be avoided through the design of master systems. Television antennas, for example, should not clutter rooftops. Master aerials to which several units can be inconspicuously attached should be developed wherever possible. Antennas should be set back as far from the edge of the street facade as reception quality will permit, and the cable should be placed in the rear of the building.

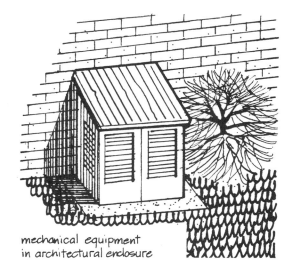

mechanical equipment in architectural enclosure

Vents and grills are out of character on the front facades and should be located in less prominent areas during the architectural planning stage. Where vents or grills are required, they should be simple in design, set flush with the surface and painted to blend with the background.

Flower boxes can give an attractive personal appearance to a residence. The box and means of attachment should appear architecturally substantial, the design should be simple and rectangular. Consideration should be given to its appearance during the non-growing season.

Whenever possible, duplication of individual utility units should be avoided through the design of master systems, for example - television antennas and solar panels.

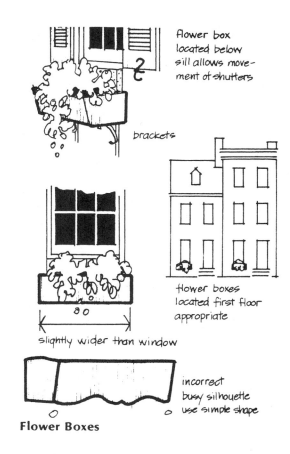

flower box located below sill allows movement of shutters

brackets

flower boxes located first floor appropriate

slightly wider than window

80

incorrect busy silhouette use simple shape

Flower Boxes

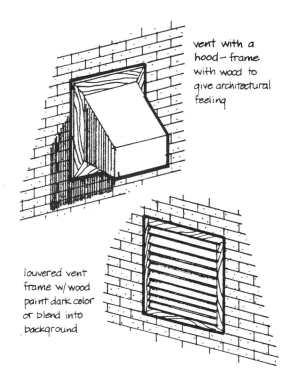

vent with a hood-frame with wood to give architectural feeling

louvered vent frame w/ wood paint dark color or blend into background

Vents

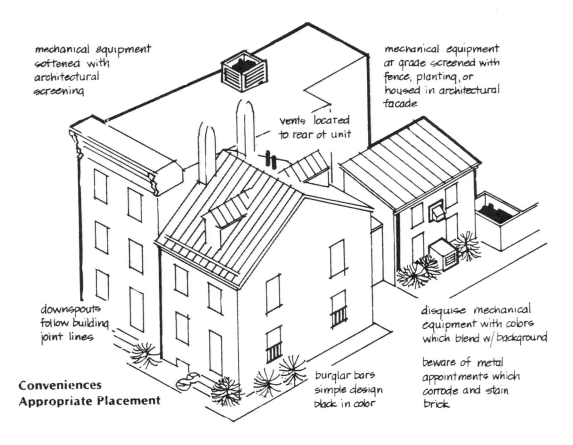

mechanical equipment softened with architectural screening

mechanical equipment at grade screened with fence, planting, or housed in architectural facade

vents located to rear of unit

downspouts follow building joint lines

Conveniences Appropriate Placement

burglar bars simple design black in color

disguise mechanical equipment with colors which blend w/ background

beware of metal appointments which corrode and stain brick

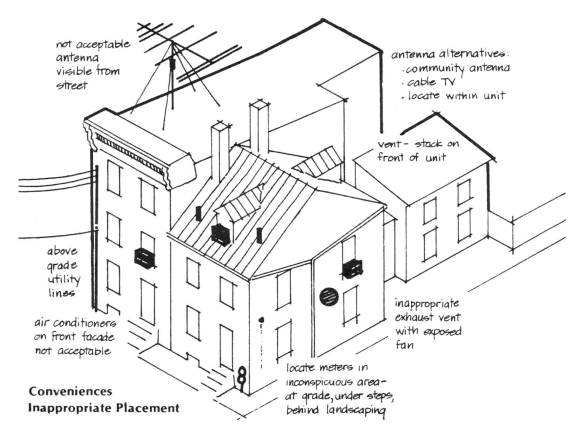

not acceptable antenna visible from street

antenna alternatives:
· community antenna
· cable TV
· locate within unit

vent - stack on front of unit

above grade utility lines

air conditioners on front facade not acceptable

Conveniences Inappropriate Placement

locate meters in inconspicuous area - at grade, under steps, behind landscaping

inappropriate exhaust vent with exposed fan

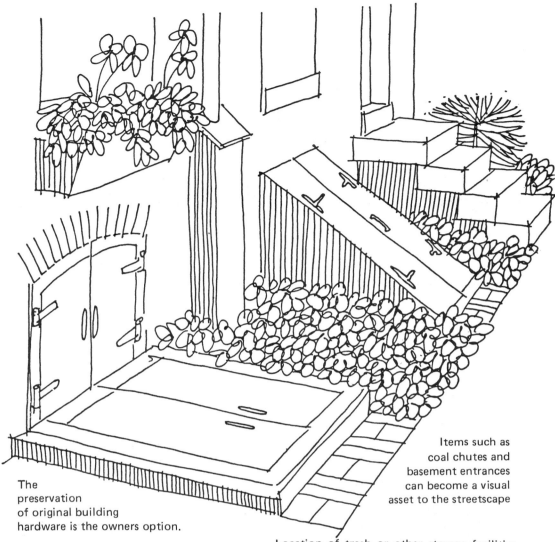

The
preservation
of original building
hardware is the owners option.

Items such as
coal chutes and
basement entrances
can become a visual
asset to the streetscape

Alternatives for hardware design -

Location in less conspicuous areas.

Using colors and materials which do not reflect a mechanical nature but do blend with surrounding architecture.

Implementing designs which are simple in nature, or follow traditional themes.

During building construction of rehabilitation, it is most desirable that central air conditioning systems be installed. Individual air conditioners on street facades are not permitted.

Vents or grills are not acceptable on front facades and should be located appropriately in the planning stage. Where vents or grills are required, they should be simple in design, set flush with the surface and painted to match the surface.

Location of trash or other storage facilities should be carefully considered with the planning of the units. Those facilities that are necessary out of doors should be clustered and made unobtrusive or as inconspicuous as possible.

Mechanical equipment on roofs should be screened and painted with a color that blends with the roofscape.

Mechanical equipment at grade should be screened with a fence, with planting or housed in an architectural facade.

Electrical lines should be located below grade if at all possible.

Avoid appointments which deteriorate quickly and require constant maintenance, for example, metals which corrode and stain brick.

Installation of utility equipment on the exterior of any building should be restricted to the rear facade or portions of the roof that are not visible from the street.

Site considerations

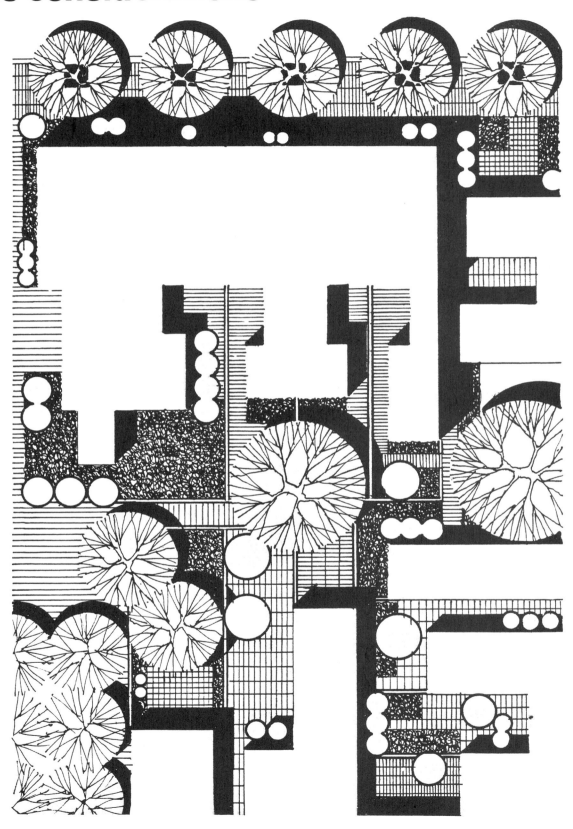

Planting

Proper site development is of prime importance in enhancing the total "image" of Otterbein. Many times important site elements are sacrificed in favor of interior architectural improvements. However, it should be stressed that proper site development is equally important in the creation and maintenance of property values.

The following guidelines for planting, fencing, walls, railings, paving and outdoor lighting are intended to provide applicable site development principles for the Otterbein homeowner.

General Planting Principles

One of the major elements in the revitalization of Otterbein will be the planting program. Plant material has the ability to unify diverse architecture, provide a pleasant environment, ensure lasting values, create shade and color, and define spaces.

It is very important that the individual homeowner's planting program(on private property) be coordinated with the overall planting program for the total neighborhood(generally on public property). A brief explanation of the public planting program follows.

PUBLIC PLANTING consists of street tree planting, open space planting, and planting along public walkways. This public program will be designed, installed, and paid for by the City. The public planting scheme will have a consistency of design and plant material and will be one of the greatest unifying elements of the neighborhood environment.

1. Large scale shade trees will be provided approximately 25' on center along the roadways and parking areas.

2. Berming and planting will be provided in the 60' wide buffer strips along Sharp Street and W. Hughes Street. The planting will probably include shade trees, evergreen trees and intermediate scale flowering trees.

3. Planting will occur in special areas of the open space such as around the community building, special gathering areas, or along the pedestrian pathway.

Even though the guidelines that follow will deal specifically with planting that might occur on private property or individual lots, an understanding of the public planting program is essential.

Residents are encouraged to coordinate their individual planting efforts with the overall public planting plan for Otterbein available through the City.

1. Appropriate varieties of plant material should be selected after considering size at maturity, location and intended use.

2. Sun, soil, water and existing conditions should be considered in selecting plant material.

3. Planting design should be simple. Planting masses of shrubbery and ground covers of appropriate scale with a predominance of one species for unity is one approach to simplicity in planting design.

4. Planting areas should relate to and complement the architectural elements of the units. For example, beds of ground cover might be designed to relate to window openings or entrance areas.

5. Planting areas shared by two homeowners should be coordinated to achieve a unified design.

Front and Side Yards

From a community standpoint the front yard of each unit is the most visually important area. Although the area is small, its design is most important and will require the most sensitivity in dealing with your neighbors and the architectural committee. The following guidelines should apply:

1. All plant beds in the front yards will be edged with a low curb provided by the City. The curbing is intended to contain plants and soil, enabling easier maintenance and enhancing the general appearance.

adjoining stoop areas or plant beds should be treated as one design

examples of various forms of planting areas to soften paving and architecture

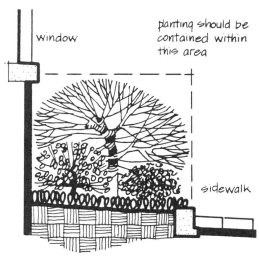

Window

planting should be
contained within
this area

sidewalk

Front Planting Zone

Federal Hill   Baltimore, Maryland

How to Make Cities Liveable

Rear Yard

The rear yards of most Barre Circle homes will be enclosed and private, offering the greatest opportunity for expression of individual tastes and needs. Even though the spaces may be small, they can be effectively utilized as outdoor rooms or gardens when carefully designed. The small garden court can serve as an amenity for a living room, a dining room, or a focus for outdoor activity.

Paving

Treatment of the rear yard areas can vary from the use of hard surface materials to the use of soft, planted surfaces. The surface treatment, of course, depends on the intended use of the area. If the yard is to be used primarily for outdoor activities, eating or entertaining, hard surfacing such as paving or decking is most appropriate. In this case, plant material is best placed in pots, moveable planters, or confined planting beds. If the back yard area is to serve as a more passive garden or extensive planted area, hard surface material may be limited to a small pathway or stepping stones.

Micro-climate

Scale, exposure, and soil conditioning are critical items in choosing plant material for the rear yard areas. The micro-climatic conditions, however, are more easily altered in the rear areas. For example, fencing or shrubbery can change wind characteristics, and trees or trellises can alter sun exposure.

Scale

Large scale plant materials, such as flowering trees or shade trees, are appropriate for rear year areas, if space or conditions allow.

Tree Selection

The choice of a tree and its placement should be done with considerable care. Remember, large scale trees not only affect shade, light and views on your own property, but also on your neighbors. Therefore, close coordination with adjoining neighbors is encouraged.

Front and Side Facade Plant Bed

Proper site development is of prime importance in enhancing the total neighborhood image of Barre Circle. Many times, important site elements are sacrificed in favor of interior architectural improvements, however, it should be stressed that proper site development is equally important in the creation and maintenance of property values. It is also evident that proper site development is a major factor in improving the micro-climate of the city.

2. Ground cover, flowers, both annuals and bulbs, and smaller, more compact shrubs are appropriate for use in the front planting areas.

3. Evergreen material is especially desirable in the front yards. Evergreens will do the best "year around" job of softening the street side facades.

4. Plants such as Barberry or Hawthorne, which may be hazardous to pedestrians or playing children should not be used in the front or side yard areas.

5. The front yard area between two entry stoops(even though divided by an imaginary property line(should be designed and treated as a total planting zone.

6. Pots or planting containers, if used in the front, should be grouped together for best appearance, not scattered about haphazardly.

7. Side yard planting should follow the same planting principles as suggested for the front yard areas.

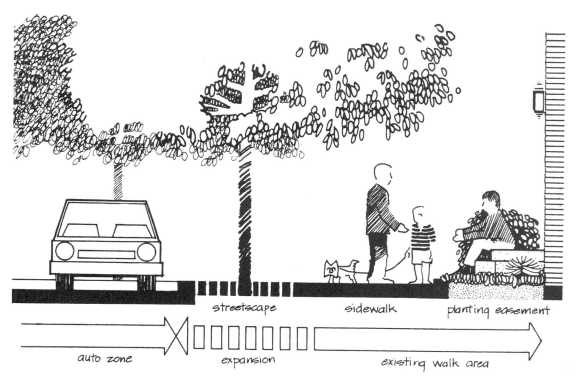

Proposed Streetscape

Paving

Much of the ground surfaces throughout Otterbein will be paved to increase usability. The front areas will be paved to allow for pedestrain circulation and the rear yards for use as outdoor rooms. The following principles should be considered:

1. In the front and side yards, all areas that do *not* require use as traffic ways or pedestrian accesses should be left for planting.

2. Where required, paving in the front easement area should be constructed of the same brick and same paving pattern as the sidewalk.

3. The extent of paving in the rear yard area should be determined by the homeowner's use requirements. Refer to the previous sketches and principles discussed under **Planting.**

4. Appropriate paving material choices for rear yard areas are wood decking, brick, concrete, flagstone, or slate. Asphalt should not be used as a paving material within these areas.

5. Paving design should be kept simple, functional, and sympathethic to the architecture of the unit. Too many materials and complicated paving patterns can create visual disharmony.

Outdoor Lighting

The outdoor lighting system for Otterbein will consist of public lighting provided by the City and private lighting by the individual homeowner. The public lighting will include street lights and pedestrian scale lights. These fixtures will be of a consistent design for the total neighborhood, providing an overall lighting continuity. Individual property owners, in determining their own outdoor lighting needs, should follow certain principles:

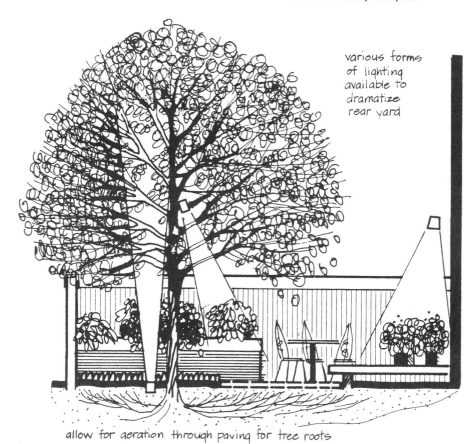

various forms of lighting available to dramatize rear yard

allow for aeration through paving for tree roots

1. The only free standing light fixtures in front of units will be street lights or pedestrian lights as provided by the City.

2. A light mounted at the entry of each dwelling unit to light steps, house number, and entry area, shall be provided by the homeowner. This fixture should provide directed light and should be of low wattage in order to prevent glare or offensive light on an adjacent unit. The entry light should be appropriate in design, color and material with the architecture.

3. Individual tastes and needs for outdoor lighting can best be expressed in the rear yard areas. However, one must not install fixtures that will cast unwanted light into neighboring properties or into adjacent units. Generally, contained or directed light sources are the most desirable, such as well lights mounted in the ground, adjustable stake lights, tree mounted "down lights" or recessed mounted wall lights.

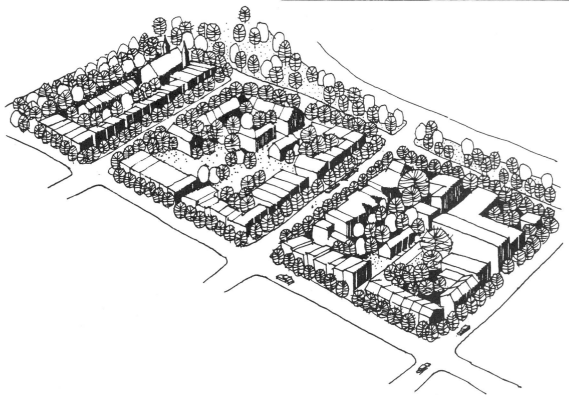

How to Make Cities Liveable

Rear Yards

The rear yards of most Otterbein homes will be enclosed and private, offering the greatest opportunity for expression of individual tastes and needs. Even though the spaces may be small, they can be effectively utilized as outdoor rooms or gardens when carefully designed. The small garden court can serve as an amenity for a living room, a dining room, or a focus for outdoor activity.

Scale, exposure, and soil conditions are critical items in choosing plant material for the rear yard areas. The micro-climatic conditions, however, are more easily altered in the rear areas. For example, fencing or shrubbery can change wind characteristics, and trees or trellises can alter sun exposure.

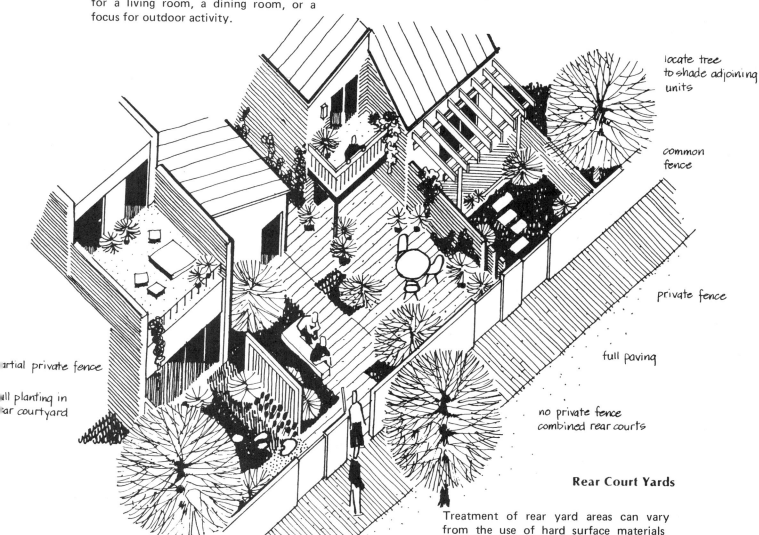

locate tree
to shade adjoining
units

common
fence

private fence

full paving

no private fence
combined rear courts

partial private fence

full planting in
rear courtyard

Large-scale plant materials such as flowering trees or shade trees are appropriate for rear yard areas if space or conditions allow.

The choice of a tree and its placement should be done with considerable care. Remember, large-scale trees not only affect shade, light and views on your own property, but also on your neighbor's. Therefore, close coordination with adjoining neighbors is encouraged.

Rear Court Yards

Treatment of rear yard areas can vary from the use of hard surface materials to the use of soft, planted surfaces. The surface treatment of course, depends on the intended use of the area. If the yard is to be used primarily for outdoor activities, eating or entertaining, hard surfacing such as paving or decking is most appropriate. In this case plant material is best placed in pots, moveable planters, or confined planting beds. If the back yard area is to serve as a more passive garden or extensive planted area, hard surface material may be limited to a small pathway or stepping stones.

Stoop
Areas

Steps and their construction will be the owners responsibility.   The owner may also add or restore coal chutes, basement windows or other original or appropriate elements in the stoop area at their own expense.

Any elements added by the owner in the stoop area should be designed so as to not interfere with access or to infringe on public right-of-way on the sidewalk.

The owner has the options of either a plant bed or paving adjacent to the unit.

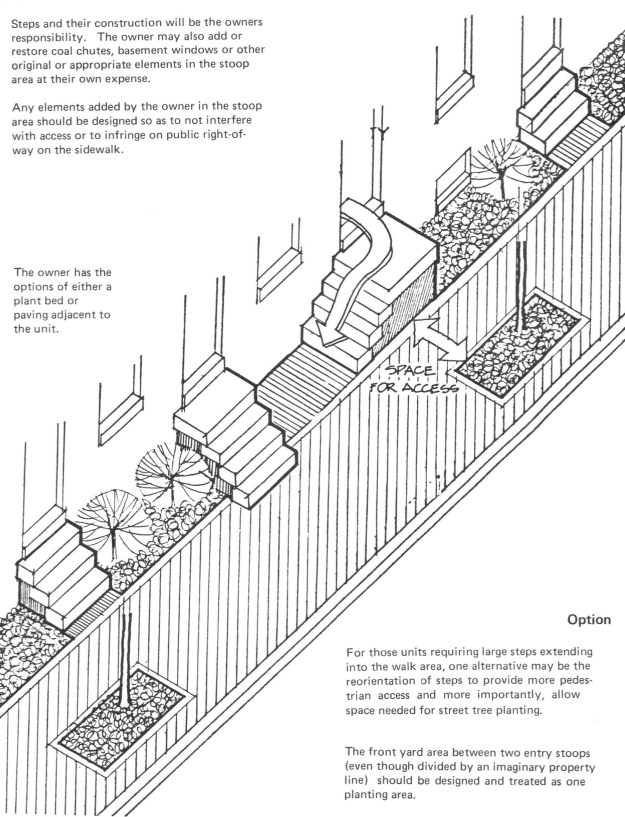

SPACE FOR ACCESS

Option

For those units requiring large steps extending into the walk area, one alternative may be the reorientation of steps to provide more pedestrian access and more importantly, allow space needed for street tree planting.

The front yard area between two entry stoops (even though divided by an imaginary property line) should be designed and treated as one planting area.

How to Make Cities Liveable

Front and Side Facade Plant Beds

From a community position the front facade is the most visually important area. Although the front plant bed area is small its impact is large and will require coordination with your neighbors and the architectural review committee.

Option

Residents have the option of either using paving or planting in the plant bed area.

Ground-Cover

Ground cover, flowers, both annuals and bulbs, and smaller compact shrubs are appropriate for use in the front plant beds.

Evergreens

Evergreen material is especially desirable in the front areas. Evergreens will do the "year around" job of softening the street side facade.

Stoop Areas

The front yard area between two entry stoops (even though divided by an imaginary property line) should be designed and treated as one planting area.

Side Facade

Side facade planting should follow the same planting principles as suggested for the front plant beds.

FRONT PLANT BED — RECOMMENDED MAXIMUM PLANT SIZES

Paving

One way to improve the urban micro-climate, is to reduce the amount of paving to a minimum. The concept of paving for reasons of low maintenance is erroneous. Paving can be expensive to install, requires repair, contributes to an unhealthy urban environment, and becomes a sign of deterioration. Paving should be used only where pedestrian traffic requires its use, otherwise appropriate landscape treatment may be more appropriate.

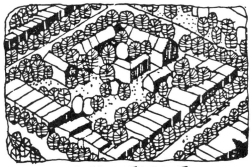

CITY WITHIN A FOREST

Options

In the front and side facade, the owner has the option of having a planting area or paving. Areas that do not require pedestrian access, should be utilized for ground cover and shrubs.

When required, paving in the front and side yards should be constructed of a masonry material, which is compatible with the sidewalk paving material.

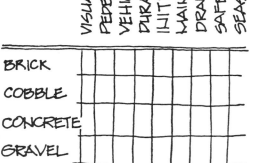

LISTED ABOVE ARE A FEW PAVING CONSIDERATIONS.

Appropriate paving material choices for rear yard areas are wood decking, brick, flagstone, concrete and gravel.

Those areas which will have vehicular traffic should engineer the paving to withstand the increased loads.

A slightly raised deck prevents soil compaction, permits more water and air to reach tree roots. Wood also stays cooler in the summer sun.

A SLIGHTLY RAISED DECK PREVENTS SOIL COMPACTION, PERMITS MORE WATER AND AIR TO REACH TREE ROOTS. WOOD STAYS COOLER IN THE SUMMER SUN.

Proper site development is of prime importance in enhancing the total neighbornhood image of Barre Circle. Many times, important site elements are sacrificed in favor of interior architectural improvements, however, it should be stressed that proper site development is equally important in the creation and maintenance of property values. It is also evident that proper site development is a major factor in improving the micro-climate of the neighborhood and the city.

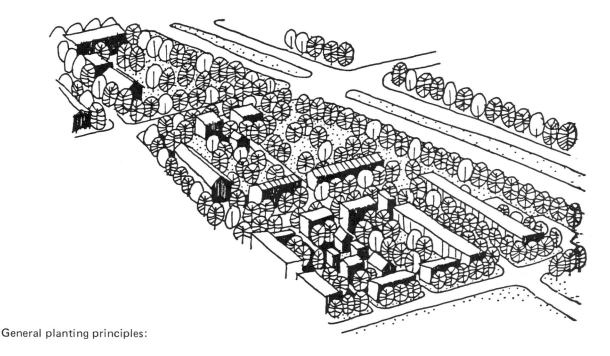

General planting principles:

Appropriate varieties of plant materials should be selected after first considering size at maturity, location and intended use.

Sun, soil, water, and existing conditions should be studied when selecting plant material.

Planting areas shared by two home owners should be coordinated to achieve a unified design.

Planting designs should be simple: planting masses of shrubbery and ground covers of appropriate size with a predominance of one species for unity is one approach to simplicity in planting design.

Planting areas should relate to and complement the architectural elements of each unit. For example, beds of ground cover might relate to window openings and entrances.

How to Make Cities Liveable

Fences

**Blockscape
and Fencing**

Unquestionably any man's fence will be shared by his neighbor, even if his neighbors have only to look at the other side of it.

**Three
Alternatives**

IMPACT ON NEIGHBORS AND NEIGHBORHOOD

Random

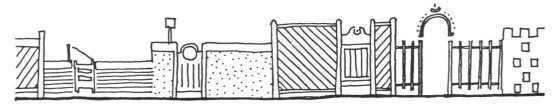

LACK OF ARCHITECTURAL COURTESY.
A COLLECTION OF DISCORDANT - MATERIALS, DESIGNS, AND COLORS.

Uniform

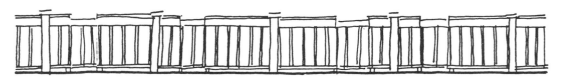

UNIFORM - DESIGN, MATERIAL, AND COLOR.
COST SAVING IF MATERIALS AND LABOR BOUGHT IN MASS.

Compatible

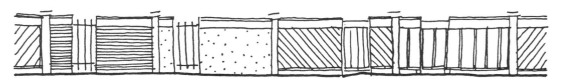

COMPATIBLE - SELECTED ELEMENTS OF FENCING WHICH ARE
UNIFORM/STANDARD THROUGHOUT THE NEIGHBORHOOD.
ex. UNIFORM HEIGHT, DESIGN DETAILS, A SELECTION OF
MATERIALS AND COLOR.

Purpose

Proper fencing can have a unifying effect upon a neighborhood, but improper fencing can only detract from the appearance of a neighborhood. Cluttering by an uncoordinated selection of designs and materials should be avoided. Cooperation among neighbors in this matter can effect the visual and psychological harmony of an area.

Selection
of Fencing

Fences as with architecture may be described and evaluated through - design, material and color. The final selection of fencing should be made according to the use it will serve(example, visual privacy, property definition, outdoor room creation). Below are some of the alternatives available.

Design

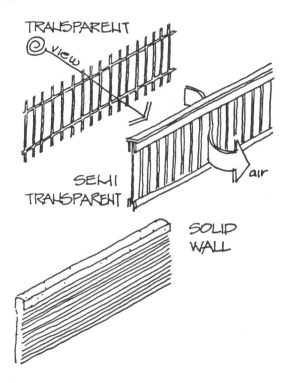

Fence designs may be divided into three areas -

transparent,
semi-transparent,
and solid.

Considerations in the use of a fence:

use of the rear court area
labor required for construction
maintenance requirements
compatibility with architecture
views and vistas off the property
micro-climate and air movement
height of the proposed fence.

Material

Three general areas of material for fencing -

wood,
metal,
masonry.

Considerations in the selection of fencing materials:

labor required for construction,
maintenance requirements,
longevity,
cost.

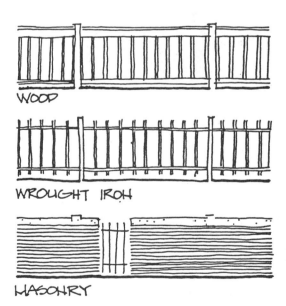

Color

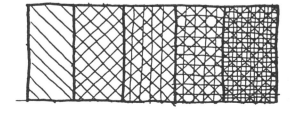

Color for fencing should be compatible with the architecture and reflect the materials used. Masonry should blend with the architecture and wood and metal color should be in harmony with the colors used in the architecture.

Fencing

Fences have traditionally been used as a physical and visual separation of two pieces of property. Fences are a notification that here one person's land begins and another's ends.

Details

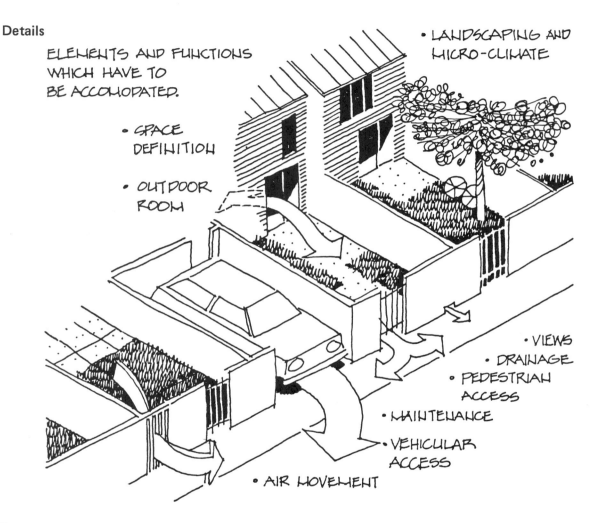

ELEMENTS AND FUNCTIONS WHICH HAVE TO BE ACCOMODATED.

- SPACE DEFINITION
- OUTDOOR ROOM
- LANDSCAPING AND MICRO-CLIMATE
- VIEWS
- DRAINAGE
- PEDESTRIAN ACCESS
- MAINTENANCE
- VEHICULAR ACCESS
- AIR MOVEMENT

Protection

Although protection applies to small children and pets, the sight of a fence can also serve as a psychological deterent to trespassers.

Outdoor Room

The creation of an outdoor room with fencing insures each person a small, private open space. Such an outdoor room can expand the interior of a house or be a separate garden or courtyard.

Architecture

Fencing can extend the architectural expression of a house.

Micro-climate

Fences also can shape the climate of a small area by creating a sheltered pocket to catch the sun or control air movement.

How to Make Cities Liveable

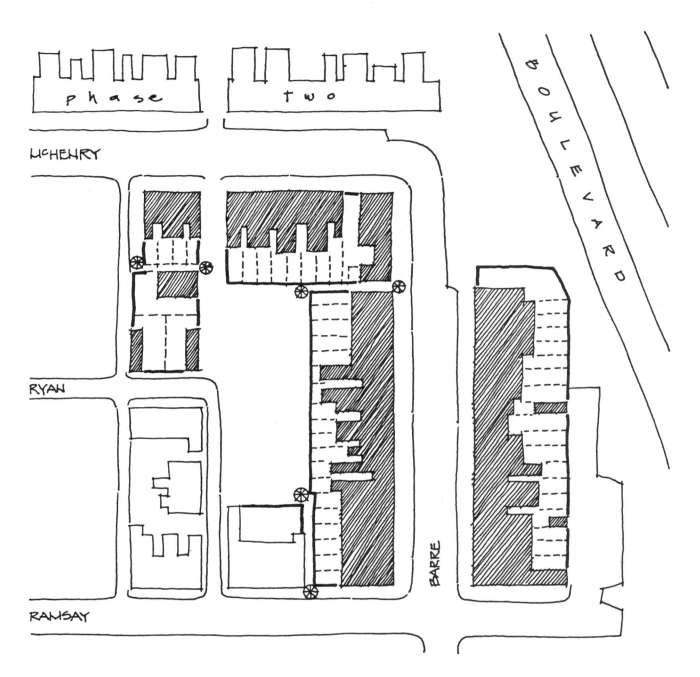

FENCING HIERARCHY
THE ABOVE ILLUSTRATES TWO CATEGORYS OF FENCING. THE
HEAVY LINE INDICATING IMAGE FENCING, VISIBLE TO THE PUBLIC
AND DASHED LINES REPRESENTING PRIVATE FENCING VISIBLE TO
ADJOINING PROPERTY OWNERS ONLY.

IMAGE FENCING
PRIVATE FENCING
POTENTIAL GATE LOCATIONS

Fences, Walls and Railings
in Otterbein

Rowhouse units, because of their small lot configurations, usually require fences and exterior walls for privacy, security and use of outdoor space. Fencing and wall in an urban situation should be considered an integral part of the architecture and thus properly designed along with house and site.

Due to the small lot at Otterbein, fencing and walls are appropriate for use along the rear yard property lines or rear building edges. In the front yard areas, only wrought iron railings will be allowed, such as around area ways or where safety or codes require.

It must be remembered that because of the closeness of units, careful consideration must be given to details, materials and colors for all fencing and walls. A sensitive working relationship between adjacent property owners is also important in their design.

Fencing Principles

1. Fencing and walls should be considered an integral part of the architectural and site design for each unit.

2. Fencing materials will be limited to brick, wood and wrought iron.

3. Brick color, size, and texture should be chosen carefully to match or complement the brick used in the house. Wood colors are limited to natural wood stains or the color used on the wood trim of the house. Wrought iron should always be black.

4. Fences or walls will be allowed in the rear yard areas only and will be a maximum height of 6'-0''.

5. Wrought iron railings will be allowed in the front when required for safety or by code, such as around areaways. Railings will be a maximum height of 3'-6''.

6. New fences or walls joined to existing buildings may require a reveal or joint to differentiate the materials and details. This may be accomplished by an offset dimension, a reveal, or gate as illustrated.

7. Fences in tight, urban situations should generally be stepped up or down to accommodate changes in topography rather than sloping with the ground.

8. Planting shrubs and clinging vines should be considered to help visually soften walls and fences.

9. Location of fences and degree of openness should take into account view or vistas, environmental concerns such as wind and air circulation, and the desired level of privacy.

How to Make Cities Liveable

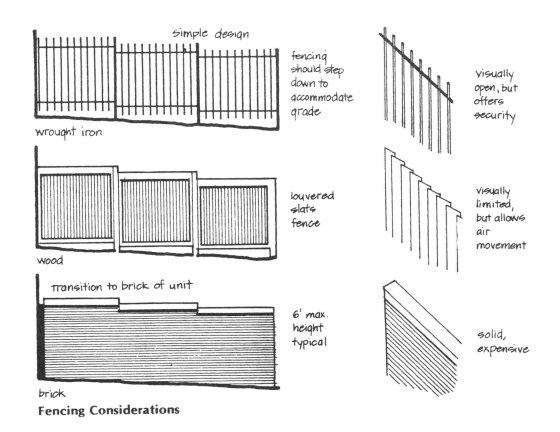

simple design

fencing should step down to accommodate grade

wrought iron

visually open, but offers security

louvered slats fence

wood

visually limited, but allows air movement

Transition to brick of unit

6' max. height typical

brick

solid, expensive

Fencing Considerations

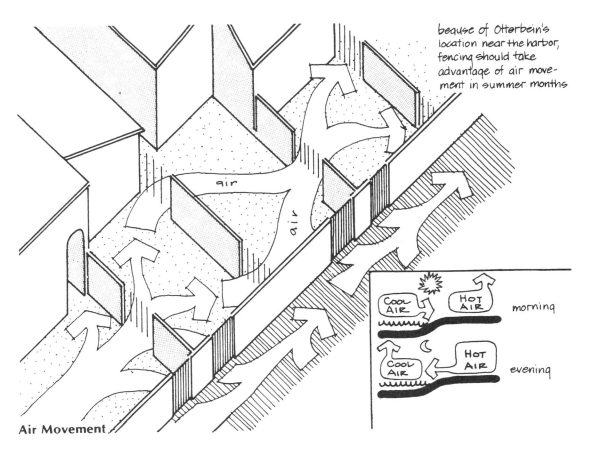

beause of Otterbein's location near the harbor, fencing should take advantage of air movement in summer months

air

air

COOL AIR   HOT AIR   morning

COOL AIR   HOT AIR   evening

Air Movement

Environmental considerations

An understanding of the effects of natural elements upon climate, on both the micro and the macro-level, is basic to any discussion of environmental considerations. Information in this area has been developed as an adjunct to studies of food production and other areas of agriculture. Historically, little research has been undertaken to determine directly the effect of outdoor environmental manipulation or control for human comfort or productivity. However in recent years society has become more sensitized to the environment and material has been developed that has direct application in this built environment. What follows is a brief discussion of some of the elements of this environment and their relationship to building in the Barre Circle area of Baltimore.

Micro-climate control

Natural elements of all types, effect the urban microclimate. The natural elements can be moved, manipulated, altered and shaped in order to control the affective climate more efficiently, effectively and completely. It is through the movement and modulation of these natural and introduced man-made elements that the site planner manipulates the perceived impact of the local microclimate as it affects people in a single building or a group of buildings.

Building design

A building design that ignores the impact of the natural environment will almost always have to use energy in the form of mechanical, structural, or material interventions to compensate for the resulting discomforts and inconveniences of adverse natural conditions. Clearly, then, a building project should start with an analysis of the assigned site or potential site alternnatives. An architect should understand and anticipate the effects of a particular site or climate on the energy flow of a building if his or her design is to use the environment to advantage.

Human comfort

Man can deal with the natural environment in several ways. Where it is hostile to his living or working needs, he can build shelters or structural enclosures to separate himself from the outdoors and its undesirable effects. He can also develop the site to minimize and economize his structural needs, in either case, his main concerns are - temperature, precipitation, air quality, sun and wind.

Site design

Architectural elements, such as fences, walls, canopies, decks, etc., may also be used to increase, decrease, direct or control solar radiation, the velocity of the wind, the amount of precipitation and humidity, and hence the temperature of specific areas of the site. The designer, during the site design phase, should answer such questions as to what architectural elements need to to be located at a specific point on the site, how high it needs to be, how wide it needs to be, of what material should it be constructed, and how it should join to adjacent materials. In essence, the architectural elements as well as vegetation and land materials should be coupled with the paving and surfacing materials as necessary to solve all of the functional problems which exist on the site, with greater emphasis on the utilization of existing solar radiation and conserving the maximum amount of energy on a particular site.

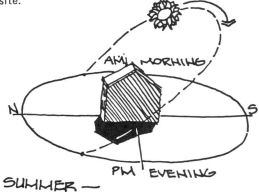

SUMMER —

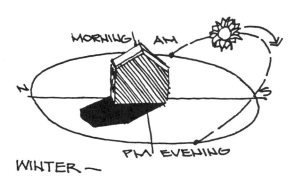

WINTER —

Solar utilization

The intensity, direction, swing, and duration of sunlight, and the effects of its direct penetration into a building, are the prime consideration. The second is to determine whether and how this energy is to be controlled or collected. Solar controls, such as internal or external shading devices for glazed areas or cooling ponds or sprays for roof areas, can help achieve maximum energy savings. But sunlight may be collected for heating, cooling, and domestic hot water needs and eventually for power generation as well.

SOLAR RADIATION AND AIR MOVEMENT

Solar radiation

As solar radiation moves toward the earth, it moves through the atmosphere before striking the earth's surface. In this movement a series of impediments cause a diminution and dissipation of the full impact of the original radiation. Some of it is reflected back into space; some is dissipated within the atmosphere; yet other portions are diffused throughout the atmosphere, a small portion of the original solar radiation strikes the earth's surface, the vegetation on the earth and buildings as well as humans and animals.

Natural elements

Natural elements, such as landforms, plant materials and water bodies, modify in a variety of ways the impact of the incoming solar radiation. As winds move over the surface of the earth they encounter a series of obstructions which defract, deflect, obstruct and lessen the impact and speed of the unobstructed wind. They do this in a variety of ways and to a variety of degrees. The effect of natural elements is two-sided - on the one hand, cutting down the impact of the solar radiation or wind, and on the other hand, accelerating or enhancing the impact.

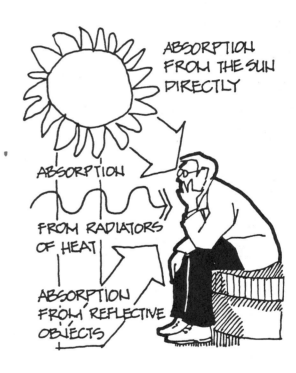

Climatic regions

The first step in understanding the effects of natural and architectural elements on the environment is an awareness of the unique qualities of the climate in the region. There are four basic climatic regions in the continental United States; these are the cool, the temperate, the hot-humid and the hot-arid. Baltimore is located in the temperate region.

Temperate region

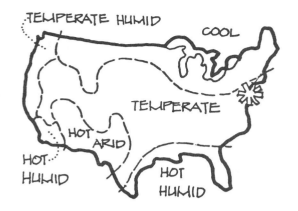

Baltimore/Barre Circle lies in the northern portion of the temperate region of the United States about midway between the rigorous climates of the North and the mild climates of the South, and adjacent to the modifying influences of the Chesapeake Bay and Atlantic Ocean to the east and the Appalachian Mountains to the west. Since this region is near the average path of the low pressure systems which move across the country, changes in wind direction are frequent and contribute to the changeable character of the weather. The net effect of the mountains to the west and the bay and ocean to the east is to pro-

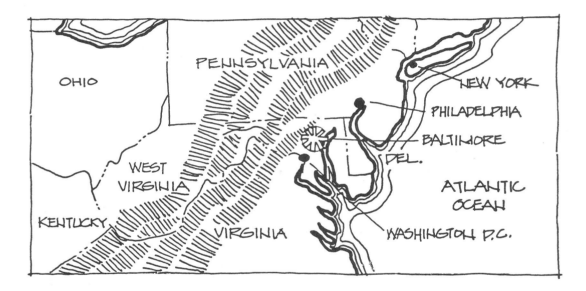

Existing urban geography

Barre Circle has a typical, hard urban environment of paved surfaces, buildings, and very little existing vegetation. It may be hot and uncomfortable in the summer, the winters are generally mild, but at times unattractive. There is pollution, noise and odor. The following are some specific areas of concern:

> high heat capacity of urban paving and
>   building surfaces,
> lack of vegetation,
> air-borne dust and pollution,
> poor acoustic properties of paving and
>   buildings,
> little retention of moisture or runoff,
> visual pollution.

duce a more stable climate compared with other continental locations farther inland at the same latitude. While hot, humid, muggy periods of weather are not uncommon during the warmer months, they are frequently attended by afternoon or evening thundershowers or night-time breezes which provide some relief from uncomfortable conditions.

The nature of urban geography

The streets and buildings of a city form an artificial rock that stores up heat during the daytime. Not only with the ground surfaces, but with all building walls and roofs equaling a surface greater than the ground plan. The building masses reduce air currents which could carry off this stored up heat. In addition, the amount of heat, which on plant covered areas is absorbed by assimilation and evaporation, remains, in the greenless urban environment.

Environmental Considerations- Barre Circle Micro-climate

The five major elements of climate which affect human comfort are - solar radiation, temperature, air movement, precipitation/humidity and pollution. A micro-climate in which these do not place undue stress upon the human body falls within the human "comfort zone".

Cities generally have a higher average temperature than the surrounding countryside.

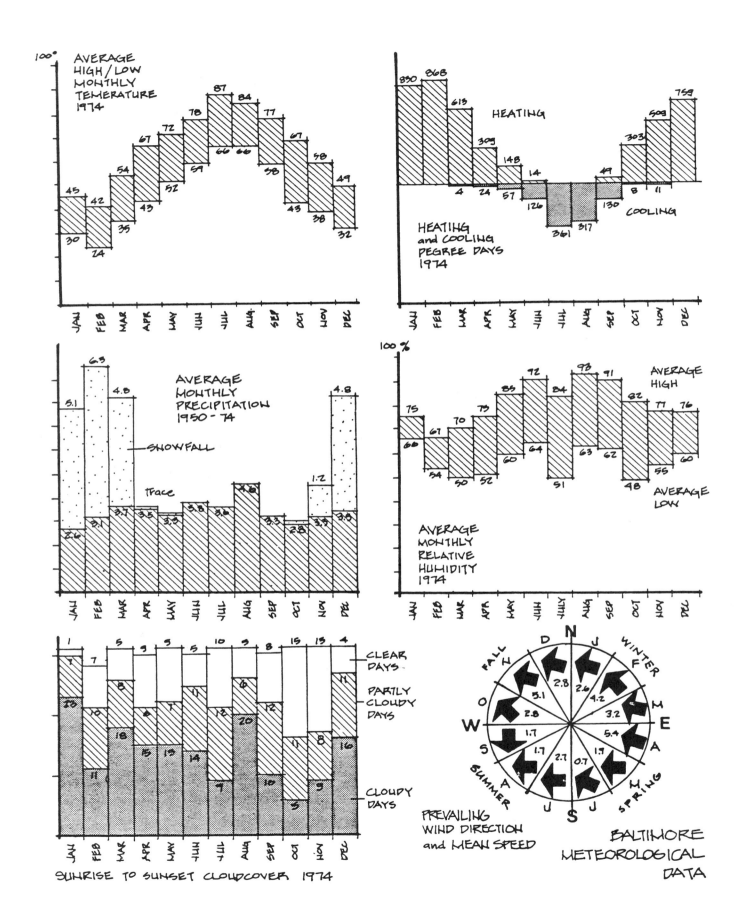

AVERAGE HIGH/LOW MONTHLY TEMERATURE 1974

HEATING and COOLING DEGREE DAYS 1974

AVERAGE MONTHLY PRECIPITATION 1950-74

SNOWFALL

Trace

AVERAGE MONTHLY RELATIVE HUMIDITY 1974

AVERAGE HIGH

AVERAGE LOW

CLEAR DAYS

PARTLY CLOUDY DAYS

CLOUDY DAYS

SUNRISE TO SUNSET CLOUDCOVER 1974

PREVAILING WIND DIRECTION and MEAN SPEED

BALTIMORE METEOROLOGICAL DATA

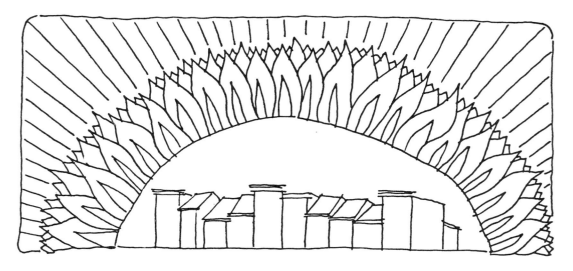

Objectives

The objectives of the environmental considerations for Barre Circle are:

1. to orient uses to maximize the positive elements of the environment,

2. to utilize vegetation to provide optimum radiation absorbant surfaces and shade giving properties.

3. to study the possibilities of creating an improved microclimate.

4. to maximize desirable summer breezes and minimize cold winter winds,

5. to minimize air, noise, and visual pollution,

6. to minimize the use of mechanical energy.

Content

When the existing site and climate conditions have been understood a determination of the type and degree of climate control necessary to provide human comfort can be made, for example a sun shade, a wind screen, a canopy to deflect rain, or a combination of these can all be used to control climate. These controls may be applied to a greater degree and a lesser degree in the outdoors. The following is a guide to some of those site and climatic conditions for the Barre Circle area of Baltimore.

The five major elements of human comfort are:

1. Solar radiation
2. Temperature
3. Air movement
4. Precipitation
5. Pollution

Solar Radiation

The sun represents two important influences to our environment. The sun is the source of the earth's climate and is an energy resource. Physically solar radiation may be either desirable or undesirable, depending on the location, orientation, season and air temperature. Harnessing the power of the sun is considered an attractive energy alternative because it is a non-polluting, renewable resource. The solar energy annually striking the roof of a typical residence is ten times as great as its annual heat demand. The following ideas suggest possible means of solar utilization in the existing urban environment in the Barre Circle area.

Solar radiation may be received as direct radiation from the sun, as reflected radiation from atmospheric particles found in the sky, or as reflected radiation from materials on or near the earth's surface.

Solar Radiation

Winter and summer sun exposure for Barre Circle

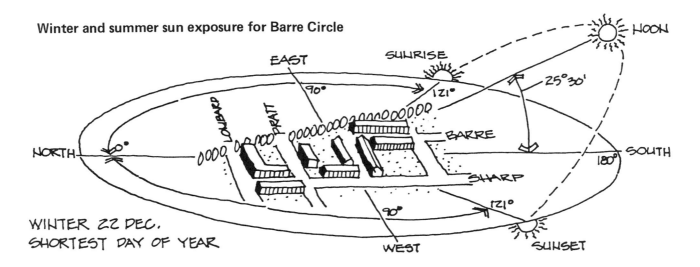

WINTER 22 DEC.
SHORTEST DAY OF YEAR

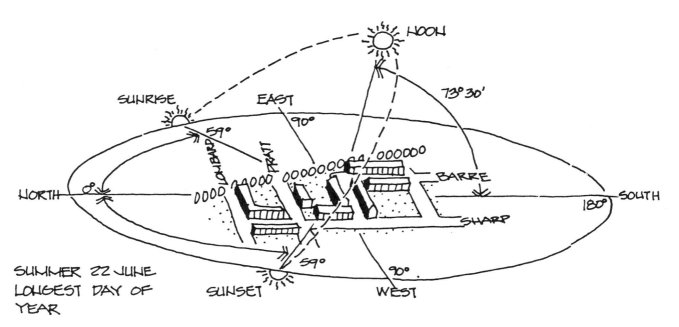

SUMMER 22 JUNE
LONGEST DAY OF
YEAR

Winter and summer solar orientation for Barre Circle

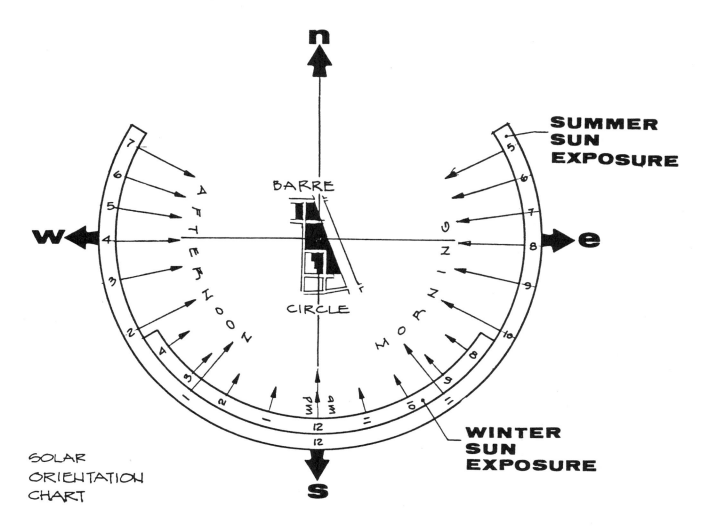

SOLAR
ORIENTATION
CHART

Solar Utilization

The south side of a structure receives the most sun, at a high angle in the summer and at a low angle in the winter. The uses allocated to the south side as well as the architectural treatment, needs to be carefully considered in order to maximize the summer exposure.

The east side of most structures will receive maximum solar radiation in the morning. In some instances, activities which would take place in the early morning time period may possibly be located to the east of a particular structure to take advantage of this radiation.

The north side of a building receives little or no sun except in the early morning and late evening, during the longest summers days. During the winter, the north facade is exposed to the prevailing winter winds from the north and west. This side of the building should be used for summer activities requiring shade, utilizing the building shadow, to minimize the need for external shade elements.

A structures' western facade will receive maximum afternoon solar radiation, and in most areas of the United States, prevailing winds are also from the west. Therefore, this area of the site requires solar protection in the summer and a certain amount of wind protection in the winter months.

Winter and summer sun angles for Barre Circle

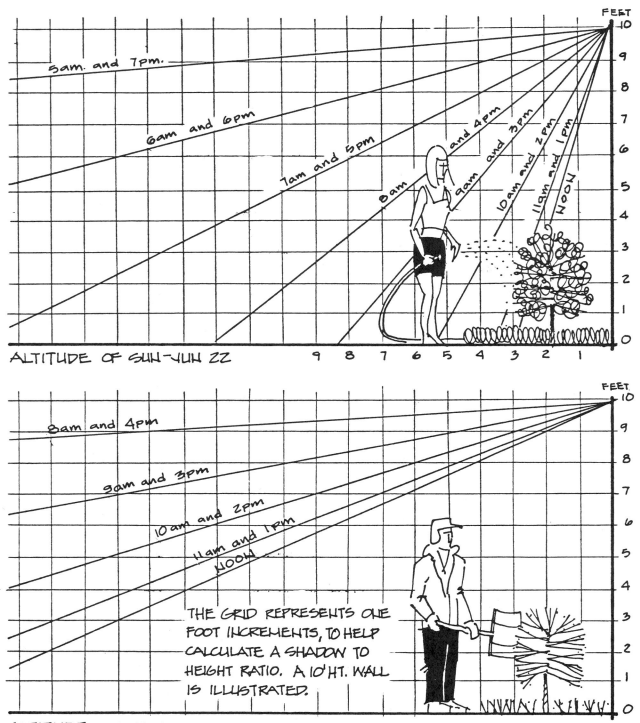

ALTITUDE OF SUN — JUN 22

5am. and 7pm.
6am and 6pm
7am and 5pm
8am and 4pm
9am and 3pm
10am and 2pm
11am and 1pm
NOON

ALTITUDE OF SUN — DEC. 22

8am and 4pm
9am and 3pm
10 am and 2pm
11am and 1pm
NOON

THE GRID REPRESENTS ONE FOOT INCREMENTS, TO HELP CALCULATE A SHADOW TO HEIGHT RATIO. A 10' HT. WALL IS ILLUSTRATED.

These diagrams indicate the angle of the sun during the longest and the shortest days of the year. The angle of the sun for the rest of the days of the year fall in between the angles indicated above.

**Use -
Orientation/Exposure
Site**

The following table shows the suggested optimum location/orientation for some basic uses in a residential unit. Although the Barre Circle units are existing and fixed in location, an understanding of the optimum may help in making decisions in how to utilize the site potential for each of the owners and indicate where protection or modification may be required.

ACTIVITY	QUADRANT ON THE SITE	FACING DIRECTION	PROTECTION FROM WHICH DIRECTION
ARCHITECTURE			
HOUSING UNIT	sw-se	s	n-w
AUTO STORAGE	e-n	n	n-w
STORAGE	e-n	n	s-n-w
SITE			
PRIME ACCESS	e-w	n	n-w
SEC. ACCESS	n	n	n-w
RECREATION			
PLAY AREAS	s-e	s-e	n-w
PASSIVE AREA	e-w	e-w	n-w

**Use -
Orientation/Exposure
Architecture**

Recommended sun orientation for rooms - This chart was developed for units with potential for windows on all sides, and again Barre Circle units are existing with the majority of the buildings having exposure on two sides only. An understanding of the following may help in developing interior layouts for optimum comfort.

	n	ne	e	se	s	sw	w	nw
BEDROOMS	●	●	●	●	●	●		
LIVING				●	●	●	●	
DINING			●	●	●	●	●	
KITCHEN			●	●	●	●		
LIBRARY	●	●						●
LAUNDRY	●	●						●
PLAY				●	●	●	●	
BATHROOMS	●	●	●	●	●	●	●	●
UTILITY	●	●						●
WORKSHOP	●	●						●
TERRACES			●	●	●	●	●	
SUNPORCH				●	●	●	●	

Control of Solar Radiation

Solar radiation may be divided into two groups of study:

- **direct radiation**
- **reflected radiation**

Control of radiation may be by filtration, by complete interception and by energy conversion.

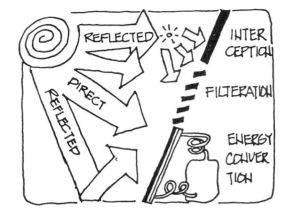

Direct Radiation

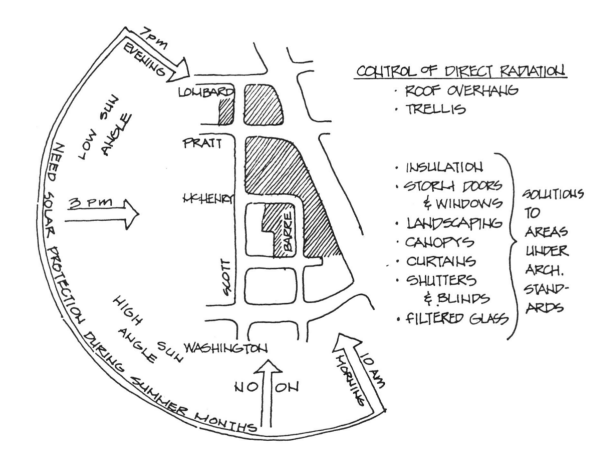

The above plan shows the direction of summer solar radiation, from mid-day through to the evening, which may require protection.

There are two major areas in the control of direct solar radiation, through architectural devices and site development methods. The following is a series of simple diagrams and notes related to control of direct radiation.

How to Make Cities Liveable

Methods of control

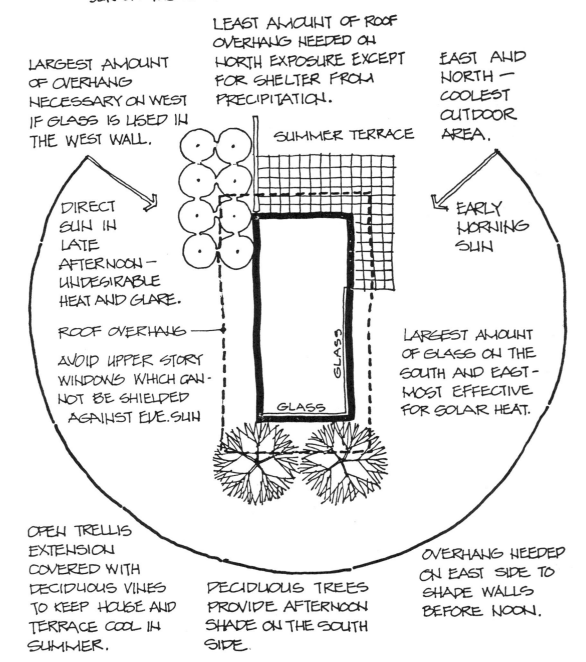

LOW BRANCHING DECIDUOUS TREES WILL KEEP LOW AFTERNOON SUN OFF THE W. AND N. WALLS.

EARLY MORNING SUN MAY BE DESIRABLE EVEN IN THE SUMMER.

LEAST AMOUNT OF ROOF OVERHANG NEEDED ON NORTH EXPOSURE EXCEPT FOR SHELTER FROM PRECIPITATION.

LARGEST AMOUNT OF OVERHANG NECESSARY ON WEST IF GLASS IS USED IN THE WEST WALL.

EAST AND NORTH — COOLEST OUTDOOR AREA.

SUMMER TERRACE

DIRECT SUN IN LATE AFTERNOON — UNDESIRABLE HEAT AND GLARE.

EARLY MORNING SUN

ROOF OVERHANG

AVOID UPPER STORY WINDOWS WHICH CANNOT BE SHIELDED AGAINST EVE. SUN

GLASS

GLASS

LARGEST AMOUNT OF GLASS ON THE SOUTH AND EAST — MOST EFFECTIVE FOR SOLAR HEAT.

OPEN TRELLIS EXTENSION COVERED WITH DECIDUOUS VINES TO KEEP HOUSE AND TERRACE COOL IN SUMMER.

DECIDUOUS TREES PROVIDE AFTERNOON SHADE ON THE SOUTH SIDE.

OVERHANG NEEDED ON EAST SIDE TO SHADE WALLS BEFORE NOON.

The above illustration indicates some of the needs and methods to improve the micro-climate relative to solar exposure.

Vegetation

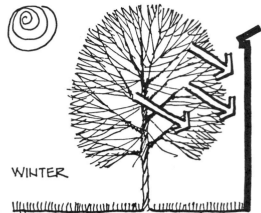

Deciduous trees can be used for summer radiation protection and allow winter sun penetration through bare branches.

Trees, shrubs, ground cover and turf are among the best exterior solar radiation control devices available and should not be underestimated. Vegetation can absorb over 90% and has the potential of reducing daytime temperature by up to 15^0 Farenheit and also raise night time temperatures by trapping warm day time air under the tree canopy.

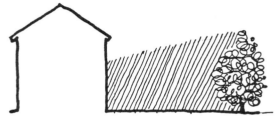

Provide protection from low morning or evening glare.

Trapping day time warmth for evening enjoyment.

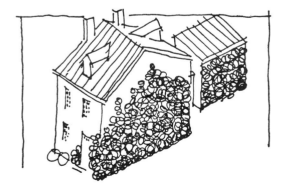
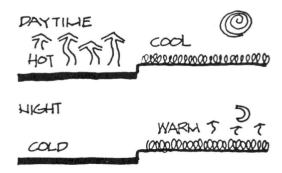

Vines can insulate and cool a house through absorption, through insulation by allowing "dead air" between the leaves, through evaporation and by providing shade.

Grassy covers tend to equalize temperature at a comfortable level as compared to the extremes of bituminous.

Urban Environment

Barre Circle is at present made of paving, dry exposed soil, and high density architectural surfaces. All these materials absorb direct and reflected radiant energy. The amount of absorbed radiant energy is compounded by the vertical construction. This absorbed energy is stored and released as heat at different rates according to the material properties.

Bituminous absorbs and quickly releases heat during the day. Brick and concrete absorb energy during the day and slowly release heat at night.

Trees

Landscaping, and trees in particular, are one of the best ways to improve the urban solar radiation problem. Blocking the radiation during the day and trapping warmth under their canopy at night will provide a more comfortable environment which is equalized throughout the 24 hours.

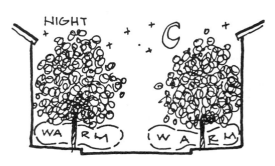

Deciduous trees also allow solar radiaiton to penetrate to buildings and pavement to provide warmth needed during cooler seasons.

Architectural devices such as canopies, trellises, and other structures are also effective but do not provide moisture, oxygen or remove pollution, as do trees.

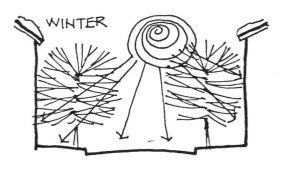

Reflective Radiation

Urbanites live in a bright and at times dazzling world with reflective paving and highly polished building materials. This glaring environment can accentuate the sun's rays and multiply the visual "busy-ness" of night time artificial illumination.

Reflected radiation affects us both visuallly and physically. The following illustrations deal with reflected radiation, its cause and effect on the urban environment and suggestions for modifying its impact.

Albedo

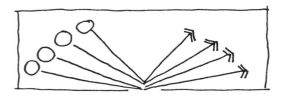

Daily and seasonal sun angles affect reflection and the amount of reflected radiation and thus the amount of absorption.

Albedo is the ratio of reflected radiation to the amount of radiation falling on the surface. The difference is absorbed and converted into heat. Materials have different rates of absorption and radiation of heat back into the atmosphere.

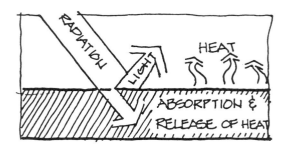

Absorption

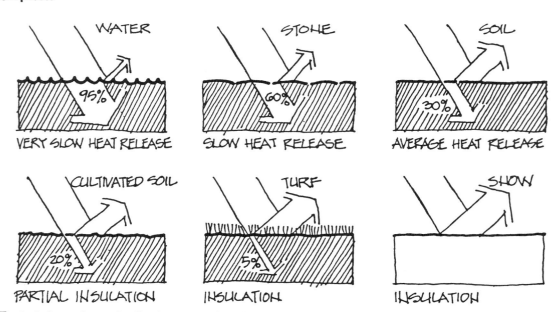

Typical absorptive and reflective properties of different substances are shown in the above illustration.

Material

Before the paving of a terrace or patio, determine the time of use/activity. An example of this would be that if the east side of a building is to be used for evening activities, then the slow release of heat as a property of brick might suggest the use of this paving material. On the other hand, certain paving materials may cause a great amount of reflection and glare when exposed to southern radiation but might be used to help illuminate an area with the indirect exposure on the northern side of a building.

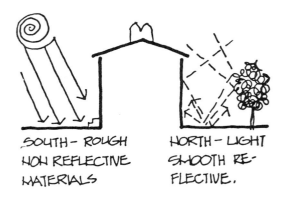

SOUTH - ROUGH NON REFLECTIVE MATERIALS   NORTH - LIGHT SMOOTH REFLECTIVE.

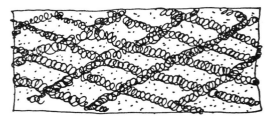

HEAT AND GLARE CAN BE REDUCED IN WALK OR PAVED AREAS BY SPACING PAVERS TO ALLOW GROUND COVER TO DEVELOP.

Color

The exterior color of a building will affect its ability to absorb or reflect heat. The lighter, smoother surfaces reflect solar energy while darker, rougher surfaces absorb the sun's light and convert it this into heat. In hot climates, buildings are light colored to reflect the sunlight and reduce heat absorption; the opposite is true in northern climates. In temperate climates where extremes in both hot and cold are common the selection of color should reflect conditions of the immediate building environment. Dark colors can be used on areas exposed to the sun if the area is shaded in the summer. Lighter colors should be used on the northern exposure to the building in the Barre Circle area to brighten and warm these areas in the early spring and late fall.

Plenum

It is possible to design or redesign a building to encourage or promote natural ventilation. A plenum, which is a sun-heated chamber, placed near the peak of a roof, a high level roof exhaust vent and a ground level intake vent are all components in this system. As air is heated in the plenum, it rises and flows out the roof vent and pulls the cooler air upward. The intake vents, if located on the north side of the structure or in other cool locations, bring in cool air, which is heated, rises and then moves out through the roof vent. This system releases hot air in the building, encourages natural ventilation and thus cools the house naturally and inexpensively.

HEATED AIR RISES AND PULLS COOL AIR INTO HOUSE

WARM AIR

COOL AIR

DIAGRAM OF PLENUM

Skylight

Skylights are an excellent interior light source for the long narrow row houses of Barre Circle. They provide sun light to interior plants and can be designed as solar heat sinks. Skylights should be sealed with chambers that transmit light but stop outward heat flow.

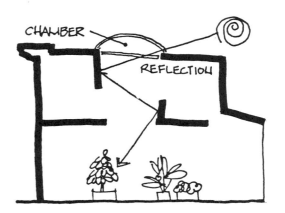

CHAMBER

REFLECTION

Rear facade

The rear facade offers more opportunity for major architectural modifications to improve the micro-climate of individual rowhouses in the Barre Circle area. Windows may be recessed to create insulating air pockets in the winter and shade in the summer. Shading devices which allow winter sun penetration yet block summer solar radiaiton may be developed for individual rowhouses along the rear facades.

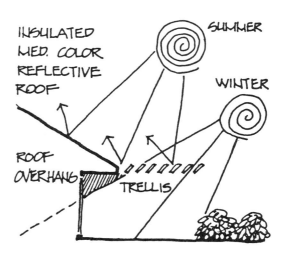

INSULATED MED. COLOR REFLECTIVE ROOF

SUMMER

WINTER

ROOF OVERHANG

TRELLIS

Air Movement

Air movement or wind can control real or perceived temperature. The air, if of low velocity, may be pleasant and desirable, however, when the velocity increases it is capable of great discomfort and even destruction to life and property. Air movement is an important element of the micro-climate and its utilization is essential.

Baltimore

Changes in wind direction are frequent in the Baltimore area because of its location near the paths of low pressure systems which regularly pass by. This contributes to the changeable character of the weather. Winter and spring have the highest average wind speeds. Summer and early fall months are the seasons for hurricanes and severe thunderstorms. Damaging hurricane winds rarely occur but winds from thunderstorms have reached 70 m.p.h. or more.

Utilization

Winds may be intercepted, diverted, or lessened by both architectural methods, such as fences, buildings, walls or other structural devices as well as by natural elements or processes, for example trees, temperature inversions, earth forms. The following are a few of the methods which are applicable in Barre Circle.

Methods of Control

There are various methods of controlling the flow of wind, from complete blockage or obstruction to filtering or channeling. The amount of blockage or control will depend on the character of the structure used to block the wind. The means of controlling wind flow or air movement may vary from land forms to various types of architecture, to walls or fences or to different types of vegetation.

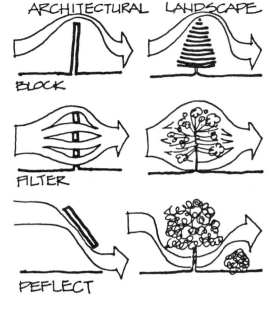

ARCHITECTURAL   LANDSCAPE

BLOCK

FILTER

DEFLECT

Windbreaks

Studies indicate that windbreaks are most effective when placed perpendicular to the prevailing winds. Wind velocity may be reduced by 50% for the distance of 10 to 20 times the barrier height downwind, depending on height, width, and penetrability of the barrier.

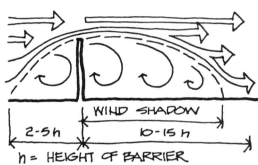

WIND SHADOW

2-5h   10-15h

h = HEIGHT OF BARRIER

Esthetic application

Wind, besides affecting our physical comfort, also acts upon our other senses. Wind passing over pleasantly odoriferous plant material can be channeled to a particular location. An acoustically stimulated effect can be gained by channeling wind through evergreen or deciduous trees. For example, wind often "whistles" when moving through a pine planting. At other times, the sound of wind moving through seed pods of honey locust trees creates a kind of natural "wind chime".

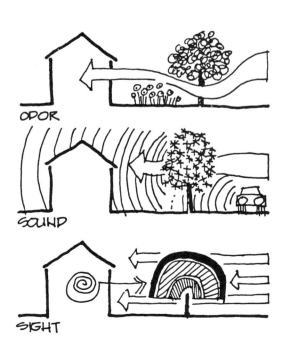

ODOR

SOUND

SIGHT

Prevailing wind

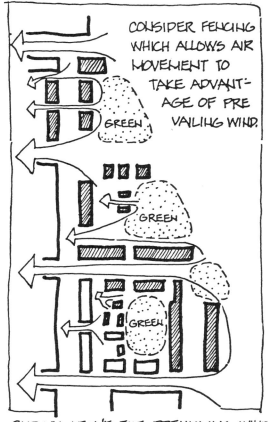

SHOWN ABOVE THE PREVAILING WIND & AIR CHANNELS ACROSS GREEN AREAS.

In urban areas, dispersion of air pollution and human comfort are largely dependent on air movement. Winds that are too rapid cause a funnel effect in urban canyon-like streets, which may lead to high air pollution through lifted street dust and strong wind fumigation from elevated sources. Lack of air movement leads to air stagnation, muggy summer conditions and high air pollution.

The ideal ventilation system would prevent the funnelling effect but favor the country breeze, i.e., air movement across cooler green areas. This could be achieved by developing properly spaced green areas and by utilizing prevailing winds.

It is also advisable to prune lower branches of all trees and to keep higher shrubs to a minimum to allow for and encourage greater air circulation.

It is possible to more fully utilize the upper levels of buildings as outdoor activity areas to take advantage of improved air circulation above street level.

It is also advisable to design, specify or install pervious or partially open fences to permit or allow greater air circulation for natural air conditioning or cooling.

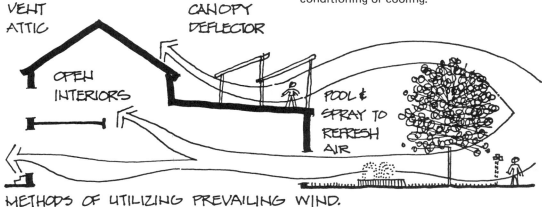

METHODS OF UTILIZING PREVAILING WIND.

Winter winds

The most significant effect of winter winds is the increase of convective cooling and evaporative cooling. The building surface exposed to those winds will require increased heating loads. At present, little is known about air movement around urban architecture, but with the knowledge that cold winter winds are out of the north and west, an assumption about which streets will become winter wind channels may be made for the Barre Circle area.

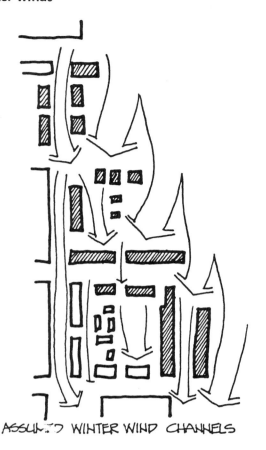

ASSUMED WINTER WIND CHANNELS

Buildings with surfaces exposed to the winter winds should keep windows and door openings to a minimum, insulate and utilize architectural and landscape architectural elements to divert the winter wind.

Landscaping

Evergreen trees, shrubs or vines or deciduous vines placed nest to a wall will create a "dead air" space between the plants and the wall. This acts much the same as the "dead air" space in the walls of a house and serves to insulate the structure inexpensively and attractively.

EVERGREENS   VINES

Architecture

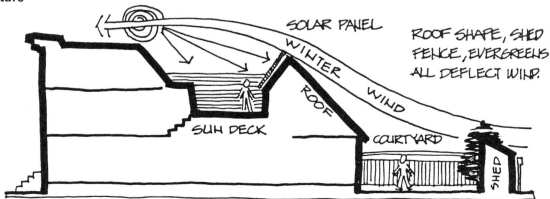

SOLAR PANEL

WINTER WIND

ROOF

SUN DECK   COURTYARD   SHED

ROOF SHAPE, SHED FENCE, EVERGREENS ALL DEFLECT WIND.

Cool air drainage

When prevailing winds are absent, two forms of local air movement become important. First warm air tends to rise, drawing in cooler surrounding air. Also since Baltimore is located near a large body of water, a sea breeze is caused by warmer air rising over land drawing cooler sea air into the city. Secondly, topographically induced night time air movement is produced by cool air draining downhill. Cool air is heavier than warm air and behaves somewhat like water flowing toward the lowest points.

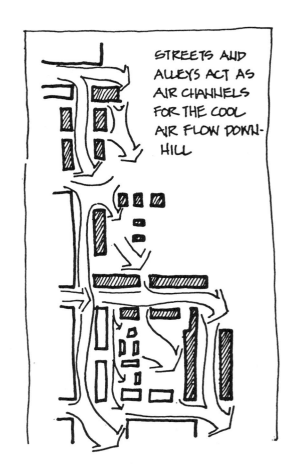

STREETS AND ALLEYS ACT AS AIR CHANNELS FOR THE COOL AIR FLOW DOWNHILL

Venting of fencing

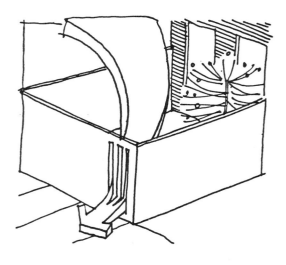

It is possible to either deflect, drain or dam cool air flow. It is recommended that for the Barre Circle area that fences and landscaping should not be designed or located to restrict cold air drainage, adequate provision should be made for cold air in the small residential courts to be drained through venting provided in the fences at the low point in the yard.

Fragrance

One potential utilization of slower moving air masses is for aroma transferral. This can be done by locating plants with attractively scented blooms such as Jasmine or Carlesi Viburnum upwind from outdoor living areas.

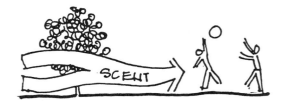

SCENT

Air and noise pollution

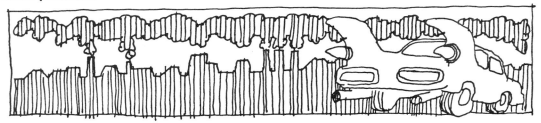

The term pollution implies some measure of contamination or impurity and may be applied to almost any subject matter   In the urban environment of Barre Circle air pollution, excessive noise and esthetic insensitivity are of immediate concern. The following section will discuss air and noise pollution; as esthetic considerations were covered in the section dealing with architectural guidelines.

Landscaping and air

Whenever possible landscaping should replace paving in the city. Technology has invented mechanical devices to clean and purify air indoors, but outdoors plants are our only effective means for atmospheric purification. The following are some of the relevant functions of plants.

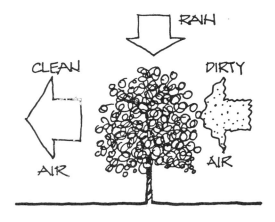

Plants transpire water into the atmosphere - in effect, washing the outdoor air in much the same way a mechanical air washer works in an indoor environment. A single Beech tree loses 75-100 gallons of water on a summer day.

Plants consume carbon dioxide from the air and produce oxygen. A 100 foot by 100 foot square stand of trees is required to supply the oxygen requirements of one person. The volume of carbon dioxide removed by one 80 foot high Beech tree equals that produced by two households per day.

Plants remove particulate pollution from the air. A street with trees may have 1,000 to 3,000 particles of pollutants per liter while a street without trees could have 10,000 to 12,000 similar particles per liter.

Plants can control fumes and odors by masking unpleasant smells and re-odorizing the air with more pleasant smells.

Noise

Noise (excessive or unwanted sound) is an increasing problem in urban areas, and has been referred to as an invisible pollution. Noise has increased to the point of threatening human happiness and health. Unfortunately there are no absolute solutions other than control of the noise at the source.

Plant materials are most effective when combined with land forms or when they are utilized to provide a "white noise" of their own which masks certain of the unwanted urban noises. An example of this is rustling leaves, rattling seed pods or the sound of wind moving or "whistling" through pine trees or pine groves.

Human comfort

There are five major elements which determine human comfort: solar radiation, air movement, humidity or precipitation and temperature. Each element tends to either offset or multiply the impact of the others.

Precipitation falls in various forms, depending on the air temperature - rain, snow, fog, sleet, hail. At the same time moisture is transpired or evaporated from the earth's surface and from the leaves of vegetation.

Vegetation

All forms of precipitation are intercepted and controlled to some degree by plants. Leaves, needles, twigs, trunks, etc. all catch, entrap, hold and filter precipitation.

Plants intercept and control the impact of precipitation to help control runoff.

Plants serve to prevent evaporation of moisture from the soil into the atmosphere while transpiration of excess water occurs through leaves, helping to equalize the temperature-humidity relationship.

Plants, especially conifers, act as dew collectors and help to control the intensity and location of fog, dew and frost.

The typical paving found around the Barre Circle neighborhood and used in walks and patios as a part of the restoration and renovation process is impervious - in that it does not allow precipitation to percolate down into the soil. All surface water is quickly drained into storm sewers. Paving should be of the design and materials which allows

absorption into the subsurface; this would take advantage of the cooling effects of evaporation and would help to replenish the ground water.

To make it drier . . .

if possible, locate activities to the south and west of the building to maximize solar exposure.

encourage and direct airflow across the site,

provide the most efficient drainage system possible,

utilize the maximum amount of paving and reduce landscaping.

To make it more humid . . .

provide windbreaks,

use extensive irrigated turf and ground cover areas,

reduce the amount of paving and hard surfaces,

utilize pools, sprays, and other water bodies on the site.

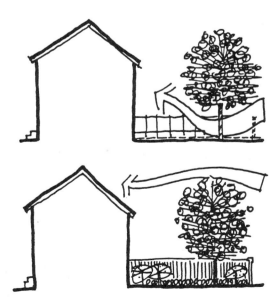

Energy conservation

In the rehabilitation of the Otterbein dwellings, a home owner should consider some basic concepts of energy conservation. Within the constraints of the existing project there are several architectural alterations that can be made to achieve greater compatibility with the existing climate, as it relates to a comfortable human environment.

Energy conservation techniques vary from region to region, depending on local climatic conditions. Baltimore is located within a temperatue region which means cold, damp winters and hot humid summers.

The basic principle of capturing as much sun as possible during the winter months and blocking out cold northern winds should be followed. In the summer the opposite should occur by taking advantage of the southern and easterly breezes and shielding out the sun.

Ventilation

Since all the buildings in Otterbein have a fixed orientation, it may be difficult to take advantage of the natural breezes for through ventilation in the summer months. End units could have windows installed on their side walls to help air flow through the structure. Attic exhaust fans can be adapted to any of the units, to eliminate summer heat absorbed through the roof. Fans can be strategically located as an integral part of the structure during rehabilitation to force ventilation through the unit and reduce the need for total air conditioning.

More than any other single element insulation will affect the efficiency of a home's heating and cooling system. Ample insulation should be provided throughout, generally 6'' in ceiling or roofs and 4'' in walls is a minimum. In addition to applied

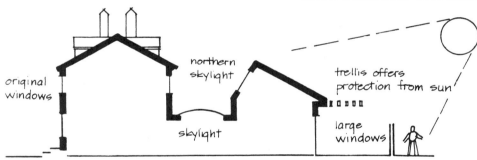

Window Orientation

Vegetation as Solar Screen

or added insulation, the building materials themselves should be considered for their porosity, color, and degree of insulation quality.

Color

The exterior color of the building will affect its ability to absorb or reflect heat. In hot climates, buildings are light colored to reflect the sunlight and reduce heat absorption; the opposite is true in northern climates. In a temperate climate where extremes in both hot and cold are common, it is more difficult to make general statements as to what is best.

In this region dark colors used on the east, south, and west will absorb winter sun and help warm the house. If the southern exposure can be adequetely shaded in the summer by using trees, trellises or extended overhangs this would present an ideal compromise. These shade producing elements not only reduce the effect of summer sun within the building, but also cool outdoor living areas.

Windows

Windows are especially important in townhouses to provide light, ventilation, and a more spacious feeling to the long narrow living spaces. However, in an urban environment, windows can also adversely affect security, visual privacy, and the climate within the home. When alterations to a facade are allowable, careful thought should be given to placement, numbers, and size of window openings and they should be functional and small.

Altered windows on the south can be large, but some consideration should be given to protection from summer sun. Serious consideration should be given to the use of insulated glass throughout.

Because of the constraints of space imposed by the existing Otterbein townhouses, it is not presently realistic to assume that solar collectors could be more than a supplementary heating source. However, the possibilities of utilizing solar energy for specific purposes, such as production of hot water, heating a greenhouse, and supplementing a conventional system are worthy of consideration.

As the cost/efficiency of solar collection hardware improves over the years, those dwellings which were initially designed to accommodate solar units will be in a better position to adapt to a future generation of efficient, inexpensive devices.

Solar energy Utilization

Orientation

The ideal orientation at this particular latitude for effective solar collection is 15^0 - $17\frac{1}{2}^0$ south-southeast. For practical application related to existing structures, it can be assumed that an orientation 10^0 - 12^0 on either side of this optimum line will produce effective results.

This orientation, coupled with a collection panel at an angle of incidence of 45^0-60^0, will produce desirable results for solar collection in both summer and winter. It is important that the panels are not shaded by trees or adjacent buildings during the peak collection hours between 9 a.m. and 3 p.m.

Installation

Because of the Otterbein architectural guidelines for front facades and roof lines, devices for solar collection should only occur on the rear or non-public side of dwelling units.

Given this criteria, some 52 single family structures in the Otterbein project area have an acceptable orientation for solar collection. An additional 14 units have a north-south orientation with their front facade oriented to the south. Many of these additional units can also be fitted for solar collection devices either through collectors on the roofs of the flat roofed units or on new additions in the rear yards.

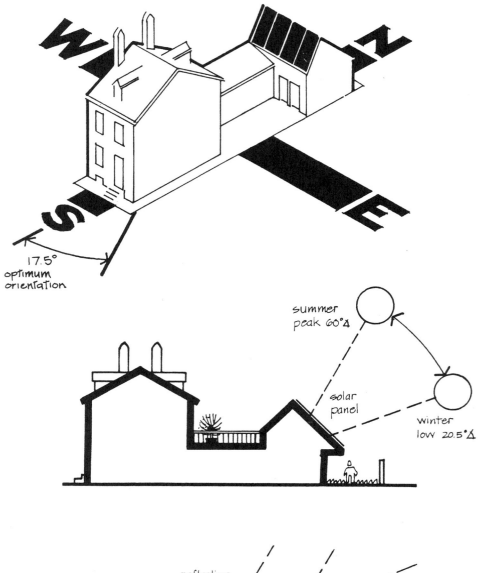

17.5°
optimum
orientation

summer
peak 60°Δ

solar
panel

winter
low 20.5°Δ

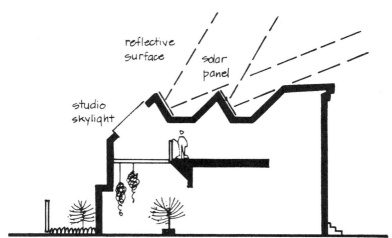

reflective
surface

solar
panel

studio
skylight

Solar Collectors

Bibliography

There are two bibliographies or lists of reference which are appropriate in this book. The first of these is the list of references which was included in the summary report for the Otterbein guidelines (the Barre Circle report contained no such list of references). The second list is a more current and general listing of pertinent sources of information on urban homesteading and ways to make cities liveable.

The following are the references listed in the Otterbein summary report:

Restoration

Davis, Deering, Dorsey, Stephen P. and Hall, Ralph Cole. *Georgetown Houses of the Federal Period, 1780-1830.* Van Nostrand Reinhold Co., 1971.

Department of Housing and Community Development, Baltimore, Md. *Design Guide - Exterior Residential Rehabilitation,* Baltimore, Md. February 1974.

McKee, Harley J., F.A.I.A., *Introduction to Early American Masonry: Stone, Brick, Mortar and Plaster,* National Trust for Historic Preservation and Columbia University, Publishers, Washington, D.C., 1973.

McKennan, H. Dickson. *A House in the City, A Guide to Buying and Renovating Old Row Houses,* Van Nostrand Reinhold, Co., New York, 1971.

Peiff, Daniel D., *Washington Architecture 1791 -1861,* U.S. Commission on Fine Arts, Washington,D.C.,1971.

Stamm, Martha and Stanforth, Deidre. *Buying and Renovating a House in the City,* Alfred A. Knopf, New York, 1974.

Stephen, George, *Remodeling Old Houses without Destroying their Character,* Alfred A. Knopf, 1974.

Waite, Diana S. (editor). *Architectural Elements - Technological Revolution.* Bonanza Books, New York.

Site Considerations

Ireys, A.R., *How to Plan and Plant Your Own Property,* William S. Morrow, New York, 1967.

The Rouse Company, *Guidelines for Residential Planting,* Columbia, Maryland, 1970.

The Rouse Company, *Guidelines for Residential Fencing,* Columbia, Maryland, 1970.

Time-Life Books, *Time-Life Encyclopedia of Gardening,* New York, 1971.

Wyman, Donald, *Shrubs and Vines for American Gardens,* The Macmillan Company, New York, 1968.

Solar Energy

Robinette, Gary O. (editor), *Landscape Planning for Energy Conservation,* Van Nostrand Reinhold Co., New York, 1983, Second edition.

The following, then, is a listing of other references which are pertinent to urban homesteading, design guidelines and how to make cities liveable.

Brambilla, Roberto and Gianni Longo, *What Makes Cities Liveable? Learning from Baltimore.* Institute for Environmental Action, 81 Leonard Street, New York, 10013, 1980.

Bronson, Gail, "The Old Homestead-Abandoned Houses are Given Free to People Willing to Restore Them." *Wall Street Jounal,* September 21, 1973, p. 1.

Campbell, Kenneth. "City Homesteading Opens New Frontier." *The Boston Globe,* July 29, 1973.

Chamberlain, G.M. "Homesteading Offers Antidote for Urban Blight."*American City,* Vol. 89, January 1974, p. 60.

Citizen's Guide to Zoning Series, Department of Community Development, 306 Cherry St., Artic Bldg., Seattle, WA 98104. February 1977.

Citizen's Handbook on Neighborhood Land Planning. John Platt *et al.*Northwest Environmental Defense Center, 11016 S.W. Terwilliger Blvd., Portland, OR 97219, 1973.

Clark, Anne and Zelma Rivin. *Homesteading in Urban U.S.A.,* Praeger Publishers, New York, 1977.

Comptroller General of the U.S., Report to the Congress.,*Urban Homesteading: A Good Program Needing Improvement,* November 13, 1979, U.S. Government Printing Office. Washington. D.C. 1980.

Corbett, Michael N., *A Better Place to Live, New Designs for Tomorrow's Communities,* Rodale Press, Emmaus, PA, 1981.

Cutler, Laurence Stephan, *Recycling Cities for People, The Urban Design Process,* C.B.I. Publishing Co., Boston, 1982.

Downs, Anthony, *Neighborhoods and Urban Development,* The Brookings Institution, Washington, D.C., 1981.

Everything You Always Wanted to Know About Planning, Zoning, Subdivision in Montgomery County Maryland But Were Afraid to Ask. Montgomery County Planning Board, 8787 Georgia Ave., Silver Spring, MD 20907, October 1973.

Fischer, Claude S., *To Dwell Among Friends, Personal Networks in Town and City,* University of Chicago Press, Chicago, 1982.

General Information: Neighborhood Conservation Program. Arlington Planning Division, 2100 North 14th St., Arlington, VA 22201. 1973.

Guide to Neighborhood Planning. Dena Wild, Project Coordinator. Department of Community Development, City of Boulder, Municipal Bldg., 1977 Broadway, Boulder, CO 80302. 1977.

"Homesteading in '73: City Houses for $1." *U.S. News and World Report,* Vol. 75, November 15, 1973, pp. 43-44.

"Homesteading Plan is Worth the Effort." Editorial. *The Philadelphia Inquirer,* October 4, 1973, p. 11.

Home, Robert K., *Inner City Regeneration, E.& F.N. Spon, New York, 1982.*

King, Wayne, "Homesteader Combating Urban Blight." *New York Times,* September 16, 1973, pp. 1,34.

Liveable Urban Streets: Managing Auto Traffic in Neighborhoods. Donald Appleyard. Federal Highway Administration, Washington, D.C. 20590. 1976. Report No. FHWA/SES-76-03. USGPO Stock No. 050-001-00111-0.

McNulty, Robert H. and Stephen A. Kliment. *Neighborhood Conservation: A Handbook of Methods and Techniques.,*Whitney Library of Design, New York, 1976.

Morley, David, Stuart Proudfoot and Thomas Burns(editors), *Making Cities Work,* Westview Press, Boulder, CO, 1980.

Neighborhood Land Use Workbook. Bureau of Planning, 424 S.W. Main St., Portland, OR 97204.

Oliphant, A. "Can Urban Homesteading Be an Idea Whose Time Has Come?" *Planning,* February 1973, p. 3.

"$1 Home Program Slowed." *The Sun* (Baltimore, Maryland), October 27, 1974. p. 15.

Ramati, Raquel, *How to Save Your Own Street,* In cooperation with the Urban Design Group of the Department of City Planning, New York, Dolphin Books, Doubleday and Co., Garden City, N.Y. 1981.

Reed, Richard Ernie, *Return to the City, How to Restore Old Buildings and Ourselves in America's Historic Urban Neighborhoods,* Doubleday and Co., New York, 1979.

The Urban Homesteading Catalogue, Prepared for: Department of Housing and Urban Development, The Office of Policy Development and Research, Prepared by: Urban Systems Research and Engineering, Inc., Superintendent of Documents, U.S. Government Printing Office, Washington, D.C. 20402, Stock No. 023-000-00415-1, August 1977.

Volume 1 - *Managing a Program, Financing Rehabilitation, Rehabilitating Homesteads, Resolving Legal Issues, Homesteading outside the Demonstration.*

Volume 2 - *Selecting Neighborhoods, Selecting Properties, Attracting and Selecting Homesteaders.*

Volume 3 - *Background and History of Urban Homesteading, Demonstration Program Descriptions.*

"Urban Homesteading." *Architectural Forum,* Vol. 139, December 1973, p. 75.

Urban Land Institute, *The Affordable Community, Adapting Today's Communities for Tomorrow's Needs.,* Urban Land Institute, 1090 Vermont Ave., N.W., Washington, D.C. 20005., 1983.

"Using Homesteaders to Restore the City." *Business Week,* September 1, 1973, pp. 22.

Wedemeyer, Dee. "Urban Homesteading." *Nation's Cities,* January 1975, pp. 19-20.

White, Anthony G. *"Urban Homesteading: A Bibliography.* Council of Planning Librarians Exchange Bibliography Number 719. Monticello, Ill.: Council of Planning Librarians, 1975.

Winslow, J.B. "Urban Homesteading: Little to Lose and A Lot to Gain."*American City,* October 1974, p. 71.

Yin, Robert K., *Conserving America's Neighborhoods.* Plenum Press, New York, 1982.

Index

How to Make Cities Liveable